ATHANASIANA SYRIACA

PART III

DE INCARNATIONE CONTRA ARIANOS; CONTRA APOLLINARIUM I; DE
CRUCE ET PASSIONE; QUOD UNUS SIT CHRISTUS; DE INCARNATIONE
DEI VERBI; AD JOVIANUM

CORPUS

SCRIPTORUM CHRISTIANORUM ORIENTALIUM

EDITUM CONSILIO

UNIVERSITATIS CATHOLICAE AMERICAE

ET UNIVERSITATIS CATHOLICAE LOVANIENSIS

Vol. 325

SCRIPTORES SYRI

TOMUS 143

ATHANASIANA SYRIACA

PART III

DE INCARNATIONE CONTRA ARIANOS; CONTRA APOLLINARIUM I; DE
CRUCE ET PASSIONE; QUOD UNUS SIT CHRISTUS; DE INCARNATIONE
DEI VERBI; AD JOVIANUM

TRANSLATED

BY

ROBERT W. THOMSON

LOUVAIN

SECRÉTARIAT DU CORPUSSCO

WAVERSEBAAN, 49

1972

Imprimerie Orientaliste, s.p.r.l., Louvain (Belgique)

D/1972/0602/11

PREFACE

This third volume of translations of *Athanasiana syriaca* contains six texts which are all spurious, but most of which had as great an influence on later theologians as the authentic books. One text (*Contra Apollinarium I*) is extant in several versions; the two complete ones have been edited and translated independently, and fragments of a third have been printed in the *Appendix*. A major difficulty in the translating of this work and of the *De Cruce et Passione* was the erratic Syriac, which is often so literal as to be incomprehensible. I have not attempted to « correct » the Syriac texts, but must warn the reader that the English translation occasionally makes sense where the Syriac does not. The problem is whether the Syrian translator always understood what he was translating. Those interested in the under-lying Greek may find these Syriac texts more useful than « literary » versions, but those who do not read Syriac may sometimes be led astray by attempts to render such distorted Syriac into comprehensible English.

As in the other volumes, the references to Old Testament quotations follow the Septuagint numbering. The translations and the Syriac texts have been divided into sections corresponding to those of J.P. Migne's *Patrologia Graeca*. For details of the Syriac MSS, of the printed Greek editions, and of the Armenian versions, see the *Introduction* to the volume of texts.

R.W. Thomson

TREATISE BY ATHANASIUS, BISHOP OF GREAT ALEXANDRIA, ON THE INCARNATION OF OUR LORD AND ON THE TRINITY.

1 Those who wish to interpret the divine scriptures in a perverse manner, wish to apply the humble words spoken concerning the humanity of the Son to his divinity, in order thereby to confirm their evil heresy. But all the truth of Christianity is found to consist in these modest words and deeds. So if they were able to hear the blessed Paul writing to the Corinthians : « You know the grace of our Lord Jesus Christ who for you was made poor, although he is rich, that you might be rich in his poverty [1] », they would never have dared to say that the Son was not similar to the Father, if they had understood what was the power of his poverty and what was the power of the crucifixion. As elsewhere the same Paul said : « That you might have the power to grasp, with all the saints, what is the height and depth and length and width of the greatness of the knowledge of the love of Christ, that you might be perfect in all the fulness of the deity [2] ». For this same reason he openly spoke through his writings also, saying : « Let me not boast, save in the cross of our Lord Jesus Christ, by which the world is crucified to me and I am crucified to the world [3] ». And again : « I judged that I knew nothing among you, save Jesus Christ and him crucified [4] ». And again : « If they had known, they would not have crucified the Lord of glory [5] ».

* And if they now had understood the divine scriptures, they would * p. 2 not have dared to say in their blasphemy that the Creator of all was a creature or created. For they are attacking us when they say : How can he be of similar substance to the Father ? For behold it is written : « As the Father has life in himself, so he gave also to the Son that he might have life in himself [6] ». Behold he that gives, they say, is greater than he who receives by a great amount. And again : « Why do you call me good, no one is good save God alone [7] ». And again : « My God, my God, why did you forsake me ? [8] » And again straightway : « Concerning the last day man does not know, nor the Son, but only the Father [9] ». And again : « The one whom the Father sanctified and

---

[1] *2 Cor., 8, 9.* — [2] *Eph., 3, 18-19.* — [3] *Gal., 6, 14.* — [4] *1 Cor., 2, 2.* — [5] *1 Cor., 2, 8.* — [6] *Jn., 5, 26.* — [7] *Mk., 10, 18; Lk., 18, 19.* — [8] *Mt., 27, 46; Mk., 15, 34.* — [9] *Mt. 24, 36; Mk., 13, 32.* —

sent into the world [1] ». And again : « The one whom the Father raised up from the dead [2] ». How therefore, they say, can he who rose from the dead be similar to him who raised him ?

2 So we have made these few remarks from a wider subject, that when these have received a solution, the rest also may be easily under- 5 stood. It is thus our duty, insofar as we are able, to expound the force of what has been said. So when the blessed Paul says concerning the Son : « The Father raised him from the dead [3] », the evangelist John tells us that Jesus said : « Destroy this temple, and in three days I shall raise it up », he was speaking, he says, about the temple of his 10 body [4]. Therefore, it is clear to those who can see that when the body rose, the Son is said to rise from the dead. For the (attributes) of his body are understood of him himself. Again in the same way, when he says : « The Father gave life to the Son [5] », it is to be understood that

* p. 3 life was given to the body. For how * is there a way for life to receive 15 life, as he promised, saying : « My sheep hear my voice, and I know them ; and they follow me, and I give them eternal life, and they will not perish for ever [6] » ? And if, again, he is the wisdom of God and he created every period of life, how does he say : « But Jesus increased in wisdom and stature [7] » ? For he is also the creator of everything. And 20 if the Father made everything through his Word, who is his Son, it is clear that he also effected the resurrection of his body through him. So through him he raises him up, and through him he gives him life. So he rises in the flesh as a man, and receives life as a man. He who was found in form as a man, he it is who raises his temple as God and 25 gives his own body life. Again when he says : « Him whom the Father sanctified and sent into the world [8] », elsewhere he says : « On their behalf I sanctify myself, that they also may be sanctified in truth [9] ». And again, when he says : « My God, my God, why did you forsake me [10] », he is speaking as in our person, because of the form of a servant 30 which he took : « and he was found in form as a man ; he humbled himself and was obedient unto death, the death of the cross [11] », and so on. As also Isaiah said : « He will bear our hurts and will accept our pains [12] ». So it is clear that not on his own account did he suffer, but for us ourselves. Nor again was he abondoned by God, but rather 35 we were ; and for us who had been forsaken he came into the world.

---

[1] *Jn.*, 10, *36.* — [2] *Gal.*, 1, *1.* — [3] *Gal.*, 1, *1.* — [4] *Jn.* 2, *19, 21.* — [5] *Jn.*, 5, *26.* — [6] *Jn.*, 10, *27-28.* — [7] *Lk.*, 2, *52.* — [8] *Jn.*, 10, *36.* — [9] *Jn.*, 17, 19. — [10] *Mt.*, 27, *46* ; *Mk.*, 15, *34.* — [11] *Phil.*, 2, *7-8.* — [12] *Is.*, 53, *4.*

And again when he says : « Therefore God also exalted him and gave him a name superior to all names [1] » * and the rest, he was speaking * p. 4 about his temple, which is his body.

3 For it was not the exalted one who was exalted, but the body of
5 the exalted one, and to his body he granted a name superior to all names. And it was not God the Word who by grace accepted to be called by the name of God, but his body with him was titled with the name of God. For he does not say that God became the Word, but : « The Word was God [2] », and thus God the Word became flesh that his
10 flesh might become in him God the Word. Just as Thomas, touching his body, cried with a loud voice and said : « My Lord and my God [3] », giving them together a divine name, in the same way John also writes : « What was from the beginning, what we have heard, what we have seen with our eyes and touched with our hands, concerning the Word
15 of life [4] ». So it is clear that it was when he was in the body that the Son and Word of the Father was touched. And both of these the divine scripture has handed down to us : « The Word of life was touched », and again it said : « The holy Spirit was not yet given, in that Jesus had not yet been glorified [5] ». For it was not the Lord of glory
20 who was glorified, but the body of the Lord of glory; this received glory when it ascended with him to heaven. Whence men did not yet have the Spirit of adoption, because the first-fruits taken from men had not yet ascended to heaven.

4 Therefore, all the things that the holy scriptures say : « The Son
25 received », and : « The Son was glorified », are spoken of his humanity and not of his divinity. And when again the Apostle says : « In Christ dwells all the fulness of the Godhead bodily [6] », * we understand that * p. 5 all the fulness of the Godhead dwells in his body. And again, when he says : « He who did not spare his son, but gave him up on behalf of all
30 of us [7] », elsewhere he said : « As Christ loved his church, he gave himself up for it [8] ».

5 For the immortal Son did not come to save himself, but us who were under the subjection of death. Nor again for his own sake did he die, but for our sake, for whom he took upon himself our meanness
35 and our poverty in order to bestow all his wealth on us. For his suffering is for us impassibility, and his death is for us immortality.

---

[1] *Phil.*, 2, 9. — [2] *Jn.*, 1, 1. — [3] *Jn.*, 20, 28. — [4] *1 Jn.*, 1, 1. — [5] *Jn.*, 7, 39.
[6] *Col.*, 2, 9. — [7] *Rom.*, 8, 32. — [8] *Eph.*, 5, 25.

father, he gave to men the immortal Father, as he said : « He gave them power to become the sons of God [1] ».

Therefore the Son of God also tasted death in the body because of his bodily father, that men might receive life spiritually in God the Father. So he is by nature Son of God, while we are so by grace. And again, he became the son of Adam by dispensation and grace, while we are sons of Adam by nature. Therefore he said : « I shall go to my Father and your Father, and my God and your God [2] ». For his Father by nature is God, as I said, whereas he is ours by grace. And he became his God by dispensation because he was made man, whereas he is our Lord and God by nature. Therefore God the Word, when he was united to the flesh, became flesh, in order that men, when united with the Spirit, might become one Spirit. So he is God clothed * with a body, and we are men clothed with the Spirit. For he received the first-fruits from the nature of men — that is from the seed of Abraham — which is the form of a servant, and he became man. He also gave us from the nature of God as first-fruits the holy Spirit, that we might all become sons of God in his likeness. So the true Lord has put on all of us, that we all might put on the one God.

9 Thus it is great impiety to say that the Spirit of God is created or made, whom all the scriptures — that is the old and the new — glorify and count with the Father and the Son; because he is of the same divinity and substance, as the Son also said : « Rivers of living water will flow from the belly of him who believes in me [3] ». This he said of the Spirit which those who believed in him were about to receive. As also through the prophet Joel, as if in the person of the Father, he says : « I shall pour of my Spirit on all flesh, and your sons and daughters will prophesy [4] ». And therefore he breathed on the faces of the apostles, saying : « Receive the holy Spirit [5] », that we might learn that the Spirit which was given to his disciples is from the fulness of his divinity. « For in Christ — that is in his body — dwells, he says, all the fulness of the Godhead bodily [6] ». As also John the Baptist said : « We all have taken from his fulness [7] ». For in the bodily form of a dove the holy Spirit was seen to descend and settle on him. So in us ourselves dwells the first-fruits and pledge of the Godhead, but in Christ all the fulness of the Godhead.

* p. 9

[1] *Jn.*, 1, 12. — [2] *Jn.*, 20, 17. — [3] *Jn.*, 7, 38. — [4] *Joel*, 2, 28. — [5] *Jn.*, 20, 22. [6] *Col.*, 2, 9. — [7] *Jn.*, 1, 16.

And let no one suppose that he receives it without previously posses-
sing it ; for he sends it from above as God, and the same again * receives   * p. 10
it below as man. So from him it descended upon him, from his divinity
upon his humanity. For Isaiah also, as in the person of the Father,
5 cries out, saying : « Thus says the Lord your God who made you and
fashioned you from the womb. Do not fear, my servant Jacob and
Israel whom I loved, the one whom I have chosen. For I shall give
water in the place of Sion to those who dwell in the desert. I shall
set my Spirit on your seed and my blessings on your sons ¹ ». And in
10 the gospel our Lord promises that he will give water to those who
journey in thirst, saying to the Samaritan woman concerning the
holy Spirit : « If you knew the gift of God and who it is who said to
you : Give me to drink, you would have asked him and he would have
given you living water ² ». And a little later he said to her : « Everyone
15 who will drink from this water will be thirsty again ; but everyone who
will drink from the water that I shall give him will never be thirsty.
For the water that I shall give him will become in him a fountain of
water flowing for eternal life ³ ». Therefore David sings a psalm to
God, saying : « A spring of life is with you ; in your light we see light ⁴ ».
20 For he knew that with the Father the Son was the source of the holy
Spirit.

10   The same he said through Jeremiah : « Two evils have my people
done : they abandoned me, the fount of living water, and they dug for
themselves broken cisterns which could not hold water ⁵ ». And when
25 the Seraphim praise God three times and say : « Holy, holy, holy, Lord
of Saboath ⁶ », they are praising the Father, Son and holy Spirit. It
is for this reason that as we are baptised in the name of the Father,
and the Son, so are we also in the name of the holy Spirit ; yet we become sons of God and not of gods. For the Father and the Son and the
30 holy Spirit * are the Lord Sabaoth, one Godhead and one power. There-   * p. 11
fore what was said by Isaiah of the Father, John applies to the Son,
while in *Acts* Paul says that it concerns the Spirit. For Isaiah spoke
thus : « I saw the Lord Sabaoth sitting on a high and elevated throne,
and the house was filled with his praising. And Seraphim were standing
35 above him, each with six wings ; with two they covered their faces,
and with two they covered their feet, and with two they flew. And

---

¹ *Is.*, 44, 2-3. — ² *Jn.*, 4, 10. — ³ *Jn.*, 4, 13-14. — ⁴ *Ps.*, 35, 10. — ⁵ *Jer.*,
2, 13. — ⁶ *Is.*, 6, 3.

of the Father. Again, when he says : « Before the heights he begat me [1] »,
he is speaking as in the person of the church, which was first created
and later born from God by grace. Therefore first is set down in
Proverbs : « The Lord created me [2] », and later : « He begat me ».

13   When, again, the scripture says : « Did not one God create 5
everything ? [3] » in the same way it is also said concerning the Son :
« Through him everything came into being [4] ». Similar remarks are
also made about the holy Spirit : « You receive their spirit, and they
die and return to their dust. And you send your spirit, and they are
created, and you renew the face of the earth [5] ». When, again, Christ 10
says to Simon about the Father : « Blessed are you, Simon, for flesh
and blood have not revealed to you, but my Father who is in heaven [6] »,
these things he said concerning himself. « For no one knows the Father
except the Son, and he to whom the Son wishes to reveal (him) [7] ». In
the same way Paul also spoke about the Spirit : « God revealed to us 15
by his Spirit. For the Spirit searches out all things, even the profundi-
ties of God. For who knows what is in a man save the spirit of a man
which is in him ? So also no * man knows what is God's save the Spirit
of God [8] ». So as the spirit of man is not foreign to him nor to his
nature, so also the Spirit of God is not foreign to his divinity or his 20
essence.

   And again, when the Lord speaks through Isaiah : « I have born
sons and exalted them [9] », in the gospel he said : « What is born of
flesh is flesh, and what is born of spirit is spirit [10] ». And again : « The
wind blows where it wills, and you hear its sound; but you do not 25
know whence it comes or whither it goes. Such is every man born of the
spirit [11] ». And at the beginning of the gospel John said : « To those
who received him he gave power to become sons of God, to those who
believe in him, who have been born not from blood nor from the will
of the flesh nor from the will of man, but from God [12] ». So all those 30
who have been born from the Spirit have been born from God; and
all those who have been baptised in Christ, have been baptised in the
Father and the Son and the holy Spirit. And again, when Peter says
to Anania : « Why did Satan fill your heart that you should defraud
the holy Spirit and cheat on part of the price of the property ? You 35

* p. 15

---

[1] *Prov.*, 8, 25.   —   [2] *Prov.*, 8, 22.   —   [3] *Mal.*, 2, 10.   —   [4] *Jn.*, 1, 3.   —   [5] *Ps.*, 103,
29-30.   —   [6] *Mt.*, 16, 17.   —   [7] *Mt.*, 11, 27.   —   [8] *1 Cor.*, 2, 10-11.   —   [9] *Is.*, 1, 2.
[10] *Jn.*, 3, 6.   —   [11] *Jn.*, 3, 8.   —   [12] *Jn.*, 1, 12-13.

have not defrauded men, but God; [1] » so he who defrauds the holy
Spirit, defrauds God who dwells among men through his Spirit. For
where the Spirit of God is, there is God. « For by this we know, he
says, that God abides in us, because he gave us of his Spirit [2] ».

5 **14** When again the scripture says : « The holy Spirit spoke in the
prophets [3] », elsewhere Paul says that the Father * spoke in the pro- * p. 16
phets : « For in all ways, he says, and in all forms God spoke previously
in the prophets; and in the last days he spoke with us in his Son [4] ».
Elsewhere it is said concerning the Son that he spoke : « Do you seek
10 trial of Christ who speaks in me ? [5] » And the Son said of the Spirit
that he speaks in the apostles, by saying : « When they hand you over
to tribunals and their congregations, do not worry how or what you
will say. For it is not you speaking, but the Spirit of your Father
speaking in you [6] ». And another time he speaks concerning the body
15 of the faithful, that they are temples of the holy Spirit, and elsewhere
that (they are) the members of Christ, and again elsewhere that (they
are) temples of God. « For you, he says, are temples of the living God,
as also God said : I shall dwell in them and walk in them, and I shall
be for them God, and they will be for me my people [7] ». And again :
20 « Whoever destroys the temple of God, him will God destroy [8] ». And
again : « You do not know that you are the temple of God, and the
Spirit of God dwells in you [9] ». For he who is the temple of the Spirit,
is the temple of the Father and the Son. For where the Spirit of God
dwells, there God dwells. And : « As the Father raises the dead and
25 vivifies them, so also the Son vivifies those whom he wishes [10] ».
Similarly it is also said of the Spirit : « It is the Spirit that vivifies, the
body profits nothing [11] ». And Paul writes to the Corinthians : « The
letter kills but the Spirit gives life [12] ».

You see that the works which are the Father's the scripture posits
30 of the Son and of the holy Spirit, as * also the blessed Apostle teaches us, * p. 17
saying : « There are differences of gifts, but the Spirit is one; and there
are differences of services, but the Lord is one; and there are differences of activities, but God is one who works all things in all men [13] ».
After saying that it is the Father who works all things in all men, a
35 little later he says that is is the holy Spirit who works all things in all

---

[1] *Acts, 5, 3-4.* — [2] *1 Jn., 4, 13.* — [3] Cf. *Mk., 12, 36; Acts. 1, 16.* — [4] *Heb.,
1, 1-2.* — [5] *2 Cor., 13, 3.* — [6] *Mt., 10, 17-20; Mk., 13, 11; Lk., 12, 11-12.* —
[7] *2 Cor., 6, 16; Ez., 37, 27.* — [8] *1 Cor., 3, 17.* — [9] *1 Cor., 3, 16.* — [10] *Jn.,
5. 21.* — [11] *Jn., 6, 63.* — [12] *2 Cor., 3, 6.* — [13] *1 Cor., 12, 4-6·*

men. « All these things, he says, the same Spirit works, dividing them among all men as he wishes [1] ».

15   Again when the blessed Paul teaches us about the holy Spirit that he is the earnest of the inheritance of our life, David posits the Lord to be that inheritance of ours. « For the Lord, he says, is the lot 5 of my inheritance and of my cup [2] ». And elsewhere : « I have called upon you, Lord ; I said, you are my hope and my lot in the land of the living [3] ». Furthermore, Jeremiah said : « He who created everything is the inheritance of Jacob ; the mighty Lord is his name [4] ». So when the prophets say of the Lord that he is the inheritance of the saints, 10 Paul posits that of the holy Spirit. « For in him, he says, you have believed and have been sealed by the holy Spirit who was promised, who is the earnest of our inheritance [5] ». By the same was Moses sealed on his face when he received the law from God ; yet none of the children of Israel were able to see him, for the light of the face of the Lord was 15 diffused over him. As it is written in the gospel : « Then the righteous will shine like the sun in the kingdom of their father [6] ».

For as the Father is light, so also is the Son the true light, and in the * p. 18 same way * the Spirit too is light, because he is from the same essence and true light. As Isaiah said : « And the light of Israel will be like 20 fire, and will sanctify him with a burning flame [7] ». But in the gospel John the Baptist said concerning our Lord : « He will baptise you with the holy Spirit and with fire [8] ». Elsewhere he said of the Lord who sanctifies : « For I am the Lord who sanctifies them [9] ». When again the the scripture calls God fire, like « God is a consuming fire [10] », in the 25 same way it also spoke of the Spirit : « There appeared to the apostles divided tongues like fire, and they sat on each one of them ; and they were filled with the holy Spirit. And they began to speak in various tongues as the Spirit gave them to speak [11] ». For all those who put on the Spirit of God, put on Christ ; and those who put on Christ, put on 30 the Father. « For, he said, this corruptible will have to put on incorruptibility, and this mortal put on immortality [12] ». For those who put on the Spirit of God, put on incorruptibility, as God is incorruptibility.

16   Again, when David says : « Many say, Who will show us blessings ? [13] » he was speaking of the holy Spirit. As also elsewhere he 35

---

[1] *1 Cor.*, 12, 11. — [2] *Ps.*, 15, 5. — [3] *Ps.*, 141, 6. — [4] *Jer.*, 10, 16. — [5] *Eph.*, 1, *13-14*. — [6] *Mt.*, 13, 43. — [7] *Is.*, 10, 17. — [8] *Mt.*, 3, *11* ; *Mk.*, 1, 8 ; *Lk.*, 3, 16 ; *Jn.*, 1, 33. — [9] *Lev.*, 22, 16. — [10] *Deut.*, 4, 24. — [11] *Acts*, 2, *3-4.* — [12] *1 Cor.*, 15, *53.* — [13] *Ps.*, 4, 7.

says : « The Lord will not hold back blessings from those who walk in innocence ¹ ». In the same way blessed Matthew also said of the Spirit : « So if you, who are evil, know how to give good gifts to your children, * how much more will your Father in heaven give blessings to   * p. 19
5 those who ask him ? ² » Luke, recounting in the same fashion, explains what the blessings are, saying : « So if you, who are evil, know how to give good gifts to your children, how much more will your Father give from heaven the holy Spirit to those who believe in him ? ³ » For if he were not from the being of him who alone is good, he would not have
10 been entitled good — which our Lord once refused to be called, when after he became man he said : « Why do you call me good ? There is no one good except God alone ⁴ ». But concerning the holy Spirit scripture does not refuse to call him good, as David said : « Your good spirit will lead me in the straight land ⁵ ». Again, when our Lord says
15 about himself : « I am the bread of life, who have descended from heaven ⁶ », elsewhere he posits of the holy Spirit that he is the heavenly bread. « For, he says, give us today future bread ⁷ ». For he teaches us by prayer to ask in the present time for lasting bread — that is future (bread), whose first-fruits we receive in this life through the incarna-
20 tion of Christ. As he also said : « And the bread which I shall give is my body, which I shall give for the sake of the life of the world ⁸ ». For the body of our Lord is the life-giving Spirit, because it was conceived through the life-giving Spirit. « For what is born of the Spirit is Spirit ⁹ ».

17 Again, when Jeremiah says of God that he led Israel in the
25 desert : « For, he says, you did not say, * where is the Lord who brought   * p. 20
us up from the land of Egypt and led us in the desert ? ¹⁰ » But Isaiah said of the holy Spirit that he led Israel in the desert. So we may hear him as he says : « He led them in the abyss like a horse in the desert ; and they were not wearied, like beasts on the plain. The
30 Spirit descended from the Lord and led them ¹¹ ». But to the Corinthians Paul said that Christ led them. « For, he says, they drank from the rock of the Spirit that accompanied them. And the rock is Christ ¹² ». And when Paul again says that he was called by him, as « God who set me apart from my mother's womb and called me by his grace, in
35 order to reveal his Son in me that I might announce him among the

---

¹ Ps., 83, 12. — ² Mt., 7, 11. — ³ Lk., 11, 13. — ⁴ Mt., 19, 17; Mk., 10, 18; Lk., 18, 19. — ⁵ Ps., 142, 10. — ⁶ Jn., 6, 51. — ⁷ Mt., 6, 11; Lk., 11, 3. — ⁸ Jn., 6, 51. — ⁹ Jn., 3, 6. — ¹⁰ Jer., 2, 6. — ¹¹ Is., 63, 13-14. — ¹² 1 Cor., 10, 4.

Gentiles [1] ». But to the Romans he said that he was called by Christ, writing to them : « In which you also are called in Jesus Christ [2] ». The book of *Acts*, however, says of Paul and Barnabas that they were called by the holy Spirit to announce Christ among the Gentiles. And what is amazing is this, that Christ said to Paul when he appeared to 5 him in the temple : « Depart hence, because I am sending you to distant Gentiles [3] ». And again, writing to the Galatians he said : « Paul, an apostle not by men of through a man, but through Jesus Christ and God his Father who raised him from the dead [4] ». A little later he also said : « I make known to you, my brethren, that my gospel is not from 10 a man, nor have I received and learned it from a man, but by the revelation of Jesus Christ [5] ». The Spirit is seen to have sent Paul and Barnabas to preach to the Gentiles.

* p. 21   ** 18** Sometimes the prophets speak in the name of the Father, as where God said through David : « Once I have sworn by my holiness 15 to David, and I shall not break faith, that his seed will be for ever, and his throne like the sun before me [6] ». And again : « From the fruit of your loins I shall set upon your throne [7] ». As also Peter said : « So David was a prophet, and knew that God was swearing oaths to him, that from the fruit of his loins — that is Christ incarnate — he would 20 set upon his throne [8] ». They also speak in the name of the Son, as where Isaiah says : « Thus says the Lord, for your sake my name is continually blasphemed among the Gentiles. Therefore my people will understand my name on that day. For I am he who speaks, and behold am come [9] ».
                                                                          25

And sometimes (the prophets speak) in the name of the Spirit, as where the prophet Agabus says : « Thus says the holy Spirit : the man who owns this strap [10] ». And again Paul writes to Timothy : « The Spirit clearly says : in the last times some will abandon the faith [11] ». And again : « The Spirit said to Philip : approach and accompany the 30 chariot [12] ». Again, the prophet Ezechiel, accusing the old people, said : « And I was grieved in all these things, says the Lord [13] ». But Paul writes to the new people : « Do not grieve the holy Spirit of God, in whom you have been sealed for the day of salvation [14] ». And again, David said of the Jews : « They angered God in the desert [15] ». And 35

---

[1] *Gal.*, 1, *15-16*. — [2] *Rom.*, 1, *6*. — [3] *Acts*, 22, 21. — [4] *Gal.*, 1, *1*. — [5] *Gal.*, 1, *11-12*. — [6] *Ps.*, 88, *36-37*. — [7] *Ps.*, 131, *11*. — [8] *Acts*, 2, *30*. — [9] *Is.*, 52, *5-6*. — [10] *Acts*, 21, *11*. — [11] *1 Tim.*, 4, *1*. — [12] *Acts.*, 8, *29*. — [13] *Ez.*, 16, *43*. — [14] *Eph.*, 4, *30*. — [15] *Ps.*, 77, *40*.

Isaiah said of them : « They were disobedient, and angered the holy
Spirit, and he was turned to hatred against them [1] ». And Stephen said
in *Acts* : « Hard-hearted and * uncircumcised in your hearts and hearing,   * p. 22
you continually oppose the Spirit of God like your fathers [2] ». And when
again Paul says of the Father : « If God acquits, who condemns ? [3] » such
things he also says about the Son and the Spirit in the same way :
« But wash yourselves and be purified and justified in the name of our
Lord Jesus Christ and in the Spirit of God [4] ». But our Lord said to
Satan about himself : « It is written, do not tempt the Lord your
God [5] ». And Peter said to Sapphira : « Because you conspired to tempt
the Spirit of the Lord [6] ».

19   And God is the one who contains everything and by whom
everything is filled, as he said through Jeremiah : « Heaven and earth
are filled by me, says the Lord [7] ». In the same way Paul also said of
the Son : « He who descended is the same as he who ascended above
all heavens to fill everything [8] ». Similarly also David said of the
Spirit : « Whither shall I go from your spirit, and where shall I hide
from before you ? [9] » His saying « where shall I go from your spirit »
showed us that the holy Spirit is the one by whom everything is filled.
« And where again shall I hide from before you ? For if I ascend to
heaven, you are there ; and if I descend to hell, you are there [10] ». Who
is he who descended as far as hell, except the Son who rose from the
dead ?

When, again, Stephen says in *Acts* : « The God of glory was revealed
to our father Abraham [11] », this was also said of the Son : « If they had
known, they would not have crucified the Lord of glory [12] ». In the
same way David also said : * « The Lord of hosts, he is the king of glory [13] ».   * p. 23
For one is the glory of the Father and of the Son and of the holy
Spirit. « For, he said, I shall not give my glory to another [8] ». For the
Son is not another God, but the Word of the one and only God, who
with the Father is given the name of Godhead, just as also the Father
with the Son is given the name of Godhead. As Isaiah said, naming the
Son with the Father : « And they will worship you and pray in you,
because in you is God and there is none except you. For you are God,
and we did not know, the God of Israel, Saviour. Those who oppose

---

[1] *Is.*, 63, *10.* — [2] *Acts,* 7, *51.* — [3] *Rom.*, 8, *33-34.* — [4] *1 Cor.*, 6, *11.* —
[5] *Mt.*, 4, *7*; *Lk.*, 4, *12.* — [6] *Acts*, 5, *9.* — [7] *Jer.*, 23, *24.* — [8] *Eph.*, 4, *10.* — [9] *Ps.*,
138, *7.* — [10] *Ps.*, 138, *8.* — [11] *Acts*, 7, *2.* — [12] *1 Cor.*, 2, *8.* — [13] *Ps.*, 23, *10.*
[14] *Is.*, 48, *11.*

you will be confused and ashamed [1] ». His opponents are those who do not confess him and his Spirit to be of the same essence as the Father, other than whom there is no God, and also those who are ashamed of his passion and poverty.

For no one can know God unless with saint Thomas they confess him who was crucified and died and rose to be « my Lord and my God [2] », who said to his disciples : « If you knew me you would also know my Father; from now you know him and have seen him. Philip says to him : Our Lord, show me the Father, and it suffices us. Jesus says to him : All this time I have been with you, and you have not known me, Philip ? Who has seen me has seen the Father. And how do you say : Show me the Father ? Do you not believe that I am in my Father and my Father in me ? And the words which I have spoken, I have not said by myself, but my Father who is in me, he does these works. Believe that I am in my Father and my Father in me. And if not, believe because of the works [3] ». The work of God the Father is to cast out demons. By the holy Spirit * he said he was casting out demons : « For if, he said, I cast out demons by the Spirit of God [4] », concerning which Luke said : « By the finger of God I cast out demons [5] ». For when holy scripture names the Son the arm of his Father, it calls the holy Spirit the finger of God. When again the scripture names the Son fountain, it calls the holy Spirit living water. And when it names the Son Word, it calls the holy Spirit the breath of God.

20   Again, the apostle said : « When he hands over the kingdom to God the Father, when he abolishes every superior and every authority and every power. For he will reign until he puts all his enemies beneath his feet. And the last enemy to be destroyed is death. For he subdued everything beneath his feet. But when he said that everything was subdued to him, it is obvious that that does not include the one who subdued everything to him, that God might be all in all [6] ». These things, then, were said concerning the subjection of creation which would be subjected to his humanity. For concerning his divine kingdom Daniel explains to us, saying : « Of his kingdom there is no end [7] ». As also Luke indicated concerning saint Gabriel, who said to the virgin about our Lord : « And he will reign for ever, and there will be no limit to his kingdom [8] ». But the apostle said that his kingdom has

*(margin: * p. 24)*

---

[1] *Is.*, 45, *14-16*,   —   [2] *Jn.*, 20, *28*.   —   [3] *Jn.*, 14, *7-12*.   —   [4] *Mt.*, 12, *28*. —
[5] *Lk.*, 11, *20*. —   [6] *1 Cor.*, 15, *24-28*.   —   [7] Cf. *Dan.*, 4, *3*; 7, *14*.   —   [8] *Lk.*, 1, *33*.

an end. « For, he said, he will reign until he puts all his enemies beneath
his feet [1] ». The blessed David also made a similar declaration, saying :
« The Lord said to my Lord : Sit on my right hand until I set your
enemies as a footstool * beneath your feet [2] ». By saying « sit » [3] he   * p. 25
5 revealed the beginning. And by « until I set your enemies » he indicated
the end. « When everything has been subjected to him, then also the
Son will be subjected to him who subjected everything to him, that
God might be all in all [4] ».

By these words he wished to indicate to us that when we have been
10 subjected to the Son and have been found to be his members, we will
also be sons of God in him. « For, he says, you are one in Jesus Christ [5] ».
Then he too will be subjected on our behalf to the Father as the head
for its members. For when his members are not subjected, he who is
head is not yet subjected to the Father, but waits for his members.
15 For if he was one of those who were subjected, he would have been
subjected to the Father from the beginning and would not have
waited for the end of time to do this. For we are those who in him are
subjected to the Father, and we are those who reign in him until our
enemies are placed beneath our feet. For because of our enemies the
20 Lord of heaven became (incarnate) in our likeness, and took a human
throne, that is David's, his father in the flesh, to build and set it up.
And after it is established we all will reign in him. when he hands over
his human kingdom to God the Father, that God may be all in all,
reigning through him as through God the Word, after he reigned
25 through him, as through a man for the salvation of all.

21   When again Peter says : « Truly all the house of Israel knows
that God made this Jesus whom you crucified Lord and Christ [6] », he
does not say of his divinity that he made him Lord and Christ, * but of   * p. 26
his humanity — that is all the church, which in him has power and
30 reigns after his crucifixion, and is anointed for the kingdom of heaven
to reign with him, who for her sake emptied himself and took her up
through the form of a servant. For the Son, God the Word, was Lord
and God ; and not after he was crucified did he become Lord and
Christ, but as I said before, his divinity made his humanity Lord and
35 Christ. When again he says : « My Father, if it is possible, let this cup
pass from me. Nevertheless, not my will but yours be done. The spirit

---

[1] *1 Cor.*, 15, 25. — [2] *Ps.*, 109, 1. — [3] *Syriac* : again (sic !). — [4] *1 Cor.*, 15, 28.
[5] *Gal.*, 3, 28. — [6] *Acts*, 2, 36.

is ready but the body weak [1]», he is thus showing here two wills, one human — which is the body's — the other divine. For the human, because of the weakness of the body, declines sufferings, but the divine is ready. As Peter too, when he heard of the passion, was fearful and said : « Spare yourself, my Lord [2]». But our Lord rebuked him and said to him : « Go behind me Satan ; you offend me, because you do not think the things of God but of men [3]».

Here too we thus understand (the matter). For after becoming in the form of a man he declines the passion. But in that he is God, he is without suffering by the nature of his divinity, and he readily accepts the passion and death. For it was not possible for him to be held by death, in that he was God. But he became (incarnate) in the form of men, and willingly died, and rose by divine power. As also David said : « Rise, Lord, and all your enemies will be scattered [4]». And again : « Rise, Lord my God, in the command you gave, and the congregation of the peoples will surround you. And for that reason you will return to the height. The Lord will judge * the Gentiles [5]». But the apostle elsewhere said : « He suffered in weakness, but lives in the power of God [6]». But the power of God is the Son, who suffered in weakness — that is through the junction with the flesh. And he declines death as a man, but lives in his own power.

22   When again our Lord says in John's gospel : « This is life eternal, that they should know you to be the God of truth, and whom you sent, Jesus Christ [7]», elsewhere the same John says that the Son is the God of truth. « For, he says, we know that the Son of God has come and given us understanding that we should know the true one, and should be in his true Son Jesus Christ ; He is the true God and eternal life [8]». So the true God is the Son, both before he became man and after he became the mediator between God and men, the man Jesus Christ. For this is what he said : « And whom you sent, Jesus Christ », who is united to the Father in the Spirit and to us in the flesh. And in this way he is the mediator between God and men. Not only is he man, but also God, as Jeremiah too said : « He is our God ; let no other be considered with him. He found all the path of instruction and gave it

*p. 27

---

[1] Mt., 26, 39, 41 ; Mk., 14, 35-36, 38 ; Lk., 22, 42. — [2] Mt., 16, 22. — [3] Mt., 16, 23 ; Mk., 8, 33. — [4] Ps., 67, 2. — [5] Ps., 7, 7-9. — [6] 2 Cor., 13, 4. — [7] Jn., 17, 3. — [8] 1 Jn., 5, 20.

to Jacob his servant and to Israel his beloved. And afterwards he was
revealed on earth, and lived with men [1] ».

But when did he live with men and was he among them, save when
he came forth from a woman and was involved in birth and growth,
5 and he ate and drank with them ? Again elsewhere the same Jeremiah
said : « His heart is profounder than all men, and who knows him ? [2] »
In the same way * Isaiah also said : « A child was born to us and a son * p. 28
was given to us; whose power was on his shoulder. And his name was
called angel of mighty council, wonderful, counsellor, great God and
10 ruler of peace, father of the world to come [3] ». And again elsewhere :
« Behold a virgin will conceive and bear a son, and his name will be
called Emmanuel [4] », which is, God with us. So he who was born from
a virgin and became a man is God. And again elsewhere he said :
« And we have seen him, and he had neither form nor fairness [5] ».
15 For he saw him first in the form of divine glory, sitting on a high and
elevated throne, when the Seraphim were praising him and saying :
« Holy, holy, holy, Lord Sabaoth [6] ». And later he sees that he had
taken the form of a servant and was in the form of men. Therefore he
said : « We have seen him, and he had neither likeness nor fairness.
20 But his appearance was more marred than a man's, and his aspect than
men. He was a man of sufferings and knowing pain. We turned our
faces from him and despised him and thought him of no account. He
will bear our weaknesses and endure our pains. And we thought him
to be harassed and the stricken of God and humbled. He is killed for
25 our sins and humbled for our wrongdoing [7] ». « Behold, God will requite
his judgement and compensate. He will come and save us. Then will
be opened the eyes of the blind, and the ears of the deaf will be opened.
Then the lame will leap like the deer, and the tongue of the dumb will
be loosed [8] ». And again he said : « Neither angel nor messenger, but
30 the Lord himself will come and save us [9] ». And David said : « Mother *   * p. 29
Sion said, a man and a man was born in her, and the Highest established her [10] ».

For this man who was born in her is the Highest, as elsewhere he
said : « And they will know that the Lord is your name, you are the
35 Highest above all the earth [11] ». When again : « The Father who sent

---

[1] *Baruch* (!) *3, 36-38.* — [2] *Jer.*, *17, 9.* — [3] *Is.*, *9, 6.* — [4] *Is.*, *7, 14.* — [5] *Is.*,
53, 2. — [6] *Is.*, *6, 3.* — [7] *Is.*, *53, 2-5.* — [8] *Is.*, *35, 4-6.* — [9] *Is.*, *63, 9.* —
[10] *Ps.*, *86, 5.* — [11] *Ps.*, *82, 19.*

defined the immutability and unalterability of the Son with a judgement. But these ones either imagine a change of the Word, or suppose
the dispensation of the sufferings to be a fancy. Sometimes they say
the flesh of Christ is uncreated and heavenly, sometimes consubstantial
with the Godhead. And then they say that instead of the inner man 5
⌐that is in us, [1] there was a heavenly mind in Christ. For he used in
the form of an instrument that which held him; for it was not possible
for him to be a perfect man. For, they say, where there is a perfect
man there is also sin; and two perfects cannot be one. And if there
were also in Christ the conflict of sin which is in us, then he too would 10
need our purification; if Christ showed in himself when he became
man that flesh which reflects and guides within us. But they say that
he took (flesh) without a mind that he might be the mind for himself
and that there be no taste of sin at all ⌐in him, [2] in the divinity and in
* p. 32 the irrationality of the flesh. * For the flesh does not sin guiding the 15
flesh — that is the reflecting [3] agent — not having previously considered the action of sin and acted through the body to complete the sin.
Hence [4] Christ was revealed by the newness of the flesh in a likeness;
but the newness of that which reflects in us, through a resemblance
and likeness and separation from sin that every man shows in himself. 20
And thus Christ is known to be without sin.

3   These are their [5] subtelties and thoughts of aberration. Nor is
their argument one; for many are the aberrations of unbelief that
are found in human reasonings. So let us first put to them the meaning
of God's will («for, (scripture) says, the Lord swore and will not 25
repent [6]») and the fulfilment of the true dispensation and the grace of
perfect help. And let us ask in return whether their thoughts agree
with the prophetic declarations, whether they are in accord with the
teachings of the apostles, whether they keep to the commands of the
fathers, whether they do not reject the explicit sayings of the Lord; 30
in order that from the prophetic declarations and from the apostolic
teachings and from the actions fulfilled by the Lord, there may take
place a confession of the truth and a refutation of the error.

So say, O inventors of your own new gospel — which other does
not exist — whence was it announced to you to say that the flesh was 35
uncreated, so that either you imagine the godhead of the Word as a

---

[1] but F. — [2] in him *om.* F. — [3] intelligent F. — [4] hence *om.* F. — [5] their
om. F. — [6] *Ps.*, 109, 4.

falling into flesh, or you suppose the dispensation of the passion and death and resurrection to be a phantasy? For as uncreated only appeared the holy Trinity * of the Godhead, eternal, [1] undeviating, unchanging. But Christ takes his origin in the flesh from men, from your brothers as it is written, and [2] is passible, and first from the resurrection of the dead, as the law previously announced. How do you say the uncreated is passible, or how do you call the passible uncreated? For you say that the uncreated being of the Word is passible, and you blaspheme against the Godhead. And by saying that the passible flesh, which was comprised of bones, blood, soul and all of our body, and became both palpable and visible [3] — ⌐that is, the body of our Lord [4] — was uncreated, you fall into two errors. Either you suppose to be illusion the showing forth and acceptance of the sufferings, like the lawlessness of the Manichaeans; or you posit the nature to be such as the substance of the uncreated Godhead. And why then do you still blame those who imagine God in human form in the flesh?

4 But you say that it became uncreated by the union with the uncreated. But hence your error is seen to be self-refuted. For the union of the flesh to ⌐God the Word [5] took place from the womb. For thence the Word, who came from heaven, established it, and it did not previously exist before the coming of the Word. It is from Mary alone, who was born from Adam, and is counted in the genealogy from Abraham and from David, with Joseph to whom she was betrothed, they both being one flesh, as it is written, not by intercourse * with each other but by generation from one (ancestor), for it is witnessed that they remained without intercourse. So Christ was born in Bethlehem of Juda, and called Joseph « father », who had the same (origin) as Mary from Adam [6]. And he was wrapped in swaddling-bands, and he was carried by Simon in the temple, and he received circumcision of the flesh according to the law, and he grew in stature.

So if he was [7] uncreated in the union, how was he not seen to be perfect in himself? But the growth of the flesh [8] took place as the Word wished [9] it. But for us to attribute growth to the uncreated is wickedness. For the uncreated is called uncreated by nature, and is susceptible of neither growth nor diminution. What is joined or

* p. 33

* p. 34

---

[1] eternity F. — [2] who F. — [3] + against the uncreated A. — [4] that ... Lord *om.* F. — [5] the godhead of the Word F. — [6] something A. — [7] is A. — [8] + who F. — [9] wishes F.

And elsewhere our Lord says : « Touch me and know that a spirit
does not have flesh and bones as I have [1] ». Not « I am » but « you see
that I have », although he is a spirit. « For God is a spirit [2] ». And
saying that he had and making proof of it, how did he say : « A spirit
does not have ⌜flesh and bones, [3] as I have » ? He did not say « I am », 5
but « you see that I have ». But this he taught, that the nature of a
spirit is something ineffable. But the sensation of the body is like
ours, which he acquired [4] for himself from the virgin, not in the way
of dispensation but by natural birth, that the body might be a body
by nature, and that it not be divisible again by the union of the 10
divinity of [5] the Word. For in this way death also occurred, the body
* p. 38 receiving it naturally, [6] but the Word * enduring it willingly [7] and
freely giving his own body to death, both that he might suffer naturally
for us and also rise again divinely for us ; since all the business of death
and birth will be seen to be for our [8] seeking and recreation [9].   15

7   Since these things are so and are confessed in the catholic church
of God, how do you again say that the body is from heaven ? And
why did Christ do this ? Speak ! Was it in order to bring the body down
from heaven to earth, and to make the invisible visible, and the non-
disgraceful capable of disgrace, and the impassible and immortal 20
mortal and passible ? And what benefit [10] would there be in these things,
O foolish ones, if [11] you say that what occurred in Christ was what
occurred in the first of creation, Adam ? Unless Christ had raised up
the fall of Adam to an incomparable resurrection, when he was revealed
in the form of the flesh of sin, and had condemned sin in the flesh, so 25
that he might also live in the flesh on earth and show the flesh to be
insusceptible of sin, which Adam had had from the first creation
without sin but by the transgression had made [12] susceptible of sin, and
had fallen into corruption and death. This he will raise up by nature
sinless, and show the Creator not to be the cause of sin ; and according 30
to the archetype of the creation [13] of his nature he raised it up, that
he might be the proof of sinlessness.

So in vain do those imagine who err and say that our Lord's body
was from heaven. Behold [14] (what) Adam brought down ⌜to us [15] from

---

[1] *Lk.*, 24, *39.*   —   [2] *Jn.*, 4, 24   —   [3] bones and flesh *tr.* F.   —   [4] reckoned F.   —
[5] of *om.* A.   —   [6] by nature A.   —   [7] by will A   —   [8] our] of us all A *corr.*   —   [9] +
concerning natural suffering A.   —   [10] profit A.   —   [11] if *om.* F.   —   [12] become F.
[13] creatures F.   —   [14] For a fragment in S see *Appendix* p. 106.   —   [15] not A.

heaven to earth, Christ took up from earth * to heaven. And behold,   * p. 39
Adam brought what was sinless and innocent down to corruption and
the punishment of death. But Christ showed it to be incorruptible and
the solvent of death; so that he might have power on earth to forgive
5 sins, and show incorruptibility from the tomb, and by his abiding in
hell might loose death and announce to all men the resurrection.
Because God created man for incorruption, and made him the image
of his eternity; « but by the envy of the devil, death entered the
world [1] ». When death was reigning over it to corruption, he did not
10 delay in becoming man. Not that he was turned into the form [2] of a
man, nor despising the existence of a man did he make a shadowy
demonstration. But he who in his nature is God, is born a man, that
in both respects perfect in everything, he ⌈might show [3] a natural
and true birth. And therefore it is said : « And God gave him a name
15 that is above all names [4] », that he might rule over heaven and have
the power to execute judgment.

8 For the creator of all appeared as the son of man; he did not
become a different man, but the second Adam, that even from the name
we might know the truth. And the apostle shows the first of creation
20 to be earlier [5] than him [6], first showing the animate, then [7] the spiritual.
But by saying « animate » and « spiritual », he does not reveal different
bodies but the same body : the first with the power and with [8] the nature of soul and therefore animate, the second with the power and
with the nature of spirit * and therefore spiritual. « For God the Word   * p. 40
25 is a Spirit [9] ». For in this way what is said of us also is to be seen, when
it is said : « The spiritual one distinguishes everything; but the animate
does not receive the things of the spirit [10] ». And behold, there is one
body of both; since that which is considered to participate in spirit
is shown to be spiritual, while that which remains with the power of
30 soul only is seen to be animate.

But why indeed, if it is as you claim, is Christ not said to be a man
only, like some new thing that has come from heaven, but to have
become the son of man ? So if on earth he became the son of man, then
behold he was born not from the seed of a man but from the holy
35 spirit, since he is and is known to be the one son of Adam who was the

---

[1] *Wis.*, 2, 24. — [2] death F. — [3] showed F. — [4] *Phil.*, 2, 9. — [5] holy F.
[6] + explanation of animate and spiritual A.   — [7] + also F. — [8] with *om* A.
[9] Cf. *Jn.*, 4, 24. — [10] *1 Cor.*, 2, 14-15.

first created. For no one else is described as the man who existed in
heaven except Adam, that he might have a body from heaven and be
understood as the son of man except for Adam. Therefore Matthew
describes him as the son of Abraham and of [1] David in the flesh; but
Luke numbers him in the genealogy as the son of Adam and of God. 5
So if you are pupils of the gospels, do not speak evil against God, but
agree with what has been written and took place. But if you wish to
say other things apart from what has been written, why do you fight
with us who have not been persuaded to hear nor to say (anything)
except what has been written? Because our Lord said : « If you remain 10
in my word, in truth you are free [2] ».

9 So how will you still be supposed to be believers or Christians,
who do not agree with the things that have been written * nor believe
the things that have occurred, but dare to define things above nature?
« Is it then a small thing for you to offer contest to men? How do you 15
offer contest to the Lord? [3] » For if those who did not believe the
prophets were condemned, how much more those who do not believe
in the Lord? For the things that he wished and desired for the eradication of sin and death, how do you dare either to say or think other
things instead? If we confess, he will also confess us; « if [4] we deny, he 20
also will deny us; if we do not believe, he will remain faithful, for he is
unable to deny himself [5] ». So what is all this measureless arrogance
of yours, that you say things that are not written and think things
contrary to piety [6] ?

You have the temerity to say that the flesh is consubstantial with 25
the Godhead, and you do not perceive that you have a double encounter
with impiety. For these things have been invented by you to say, in
order that you either deny the flesh or blaspheme against the Godhead,
as you say : We say that he who (was born) of Mary is consubstantial
with the Father. These fine words, as you suppose, will be seen to be 30
either perversity or senseless. But what believer will not confess that
God the Word, who came, came forth as a man from the holy [7] virgin
Mary, and although consubstantial with the Father, became man
from the seed of Abraham, whose son he was called, and (that) the
Word consubstantial with the Father became the son of David in the 35
flesh? Therefore the prophets and apostles and evangelists reckon

* p. 41

---

[1] of *om.* F. — [2] *Jn., 8, 36.* — [3] *Is., 7, 13* — [4] and if F — [5] *2 Tim., 2, 12-13.*
[6] + concerning consubstantial A. — [7] holy *om.* A.

⌐Christ's * genealogy ¹ in the flesh ⌐from the seed ² of David. So how   * p. 42
are you not ashamed when you say these things, indicating that the
flesh ³, which is reckoned in the genealogies to be from the seed of
David, is consubstantial with the Word?

5   Or again, as we said, you say these things irrationally, not understanding that « consubstantial» has indivisible equality of nature,
and exhibits in itself its own perfection. For as when the Son is confessed
to be consubstantial with the Father, perfect is confessed with regard
to perfect, likewise also the holy Spirit; for the holy Trinity is consub-
10 stantial. So give to the consubstantial flesh perfection in addition to the
perfection of the Word, and there will be according to your argument
a quaternity preached instead of the Trinity. And what is all this
invention of wickedness?

10 But you say that the flesh became consubstantial with the
15 Word. How did it become consubstantial? Speak! It became the
Word, yet became spirit. But if what is not by nature godhead becomes
godhead by transformation, why do you reprove the Arians who
propound this opinion about the Word? And behold scripture said :
« The Word became flesh ⁴», not the flesh became the Word. It is said
20 that the Word became flesh because it was the Word's flesh and not
any man's. That is, God became man. And it is said that he became
flesh, lest you should omit the name of the flesh. So if the natural
unconfused union that the Word had with his flesh does not suffice
for you, and that he is God and also became man, now you do not
25 wish to hear or believe, nor are you satisfied * to hear the body of God   * p. 43
to be above all notion of praise, like he who said : « ⌐He will transform ⁵
the form of the body of our humility into the likeness of ⁶ the body of
his glory ⁷ », which is an indication of the world to come. And again it
is called the body of his glory. But our Lord says : « When the son of
30 man will come ⁸». He said that God became the son of man, and is
judge of the living and the dead, and king and Lord and ⌐God of
truth ⁹.

But you wish to take away the name of the body or still to call
Christ a man. How are you still able to read the holy scriptures, when
35 Matthew writes : « The book of the birth of Jesus Christ, son of David,

---

¹ Christ F — ² (as) the son F. — ³ son F. — ⁴ *Jn.*, 1, *14.* — ⁵ he who will
transform F. — ⁶ and A — ⁷ *Phil.*, 3, *21.* — ⁸ *Mk.*, 8, *38.* — ⁹ true God F.

son of Abraham [1]». And John : « In the beginning was the Word, and the Word was with God, and the Word was God [2] ». If you wish to examine separately God the Word and the son of David, there would consequently be two named according to your argument. But if you 5 believe, being instructed by the holy scriptures, that although he is God, the Word became the son of man, (then) you can recognise that Christ is one, both God and man, one and the same ; that the double preaching of his coming might have easily demonstrable persuasiveness of the suffering and impassibility. As when the apostle says : « The man 10 Jesus Christ who gave himself for us, who is God blessed above all for ever and ever, Amen [3] ». And writing to Timothy, he says : * p. 44 « Remember Jesus Christ, who rose from the dead, * from the seed of David [4] ». And he again said : « We preach his death until he comes [5] ».

11   So if by the confession of « consubstantial » you are taking away 15 the name of the flesh and the fact that Christ is called a man, no longer do you preach his death until he comes, suppressing the scriptures [6]. Or preaching the death against the « consubstantial with the Father and the holy Spirit », as you do not confess that Christ suffered in the flesh, you both say that the godhead of the Father and of the 20 holy Spirit is susceptible of death, and become more wicked than all the heretics. For the death of the flesh was that of the consubstantial Word. For the Father did not put on the body, nor did the holy Spirit, as those of the party of Valentinus imagine in their wickedness. But « the Word became flesh [7] ». Therefore we, confessing Christ to be 25 God and man, do not say these things because of the separation — far from it ! — but again according to the scriptures, in order to confess that the passion and death, that occurred and were preached until he should come, to be passion and death with respect to the flesh of the Word, but that we believe the Word [8] himself to be immutable and 30 unchangeable [9]. Therefore it is the same who suffered and did not suffer. In the nature of the godhead he is impassible and immutable and unchangeable ; but in the flesh he suffered, as Peter says : « So Christ suffered for us in the flesh [10] ». And he tasted death in the flesh, and became « mediator between God and men, the man Christ Jesus, 35

---

[1] *Mt.*, 1, 1. — [2] *Jn.*, 1, 1. — [3] *1 Tim.*, 2, 5-6; *Rom.*, 9, 5. — [4] *2 Tim.*, 2, 8. — [5] *1 Cor.*, 11, 26. — [6] scripture F. — [7] *Jn.*, 1, 14. — [8] death A. — [9] + passible in the flesh A. — [10] *1 Pet.*, 4, 1.

who gave himself for salvation on our behalf [1] ». * And again : « There is   * p. 45
no mediator for one person; but God is one [2] ».

12   Therefore they are in error who say that the Son who suffered
is one, and another he who did not suffer. For it is no other than
5 the Son of God who accepted suffering and death. But the impassible
and incorporeal Word submitted to the birth of human flesh, and
fulfilled everything, in order to have something to offer on our behalf.
And it is said that « he became superior to the angels [3] », not that the
Word the creator of the angels became superior, as if he was at some
10 time inferior; but the form of a servant, which the Word made his own
by a natural birth, was made superior when he was made manifest by
the birth from the first created; and he associates [4] us, as it is written,
« as we become citizens of the saints and associates of God [5] ». And it
became by nature God's own, not since the flesh is consubstantial with
15 the godhead of the Word, as co-eternal, but it became his own by nature
and indivisible by the union, from the seed of David and of Abraham
and of Adam, from whom we also are born.

But if the flesh were consubstantial with the Word and co-eternal,
if you said this, then all creatures also would be co-eternal with God
20 who created everything. And how are they still Christians who are
entwined in these perversities ? For [6] what is consubstantial with the
Word, impassible and unsusceptible of death [7], is not capable of a
consubstantial union by hypostasis but of one by nature; but by
hypostasis it receives its own perfection. Thus by your invention
25 — which is supposed *to be reverent — either you deny the flesh from   * p. 46
the virgin mother of God, or you blaspheme the divinity. But if you
thus confess the Son to be consubstantial with the Father and the
holy Spirit, as the flesh which suffered, why do you still blame us for
saying a quaternity instead of a trinity, when you yourselves, although
30 unwillingly, confess a quaternity instead of a trinity, saying that the
flesh is consubstantial with the trinity ?

So your faith is vain. For you have thoughts like those of the wicked
Arians, since you wickedly interpret « the Word became flesh ». For
the Word became flesh, not that the Word might no longer be Word,
35 but that the Word might be in the flesh. But the Word became flesh
that both the Word might be Word and also the Word might also have

---

[1] *1 Tim.*, 2, 5-6. — [2] *Gal.*, 3, 20. — [3] *Heb.*, 1, 4. — [4] associated F. —
[5] *Eph.*, 2, 19. — [6] for *om.* A. — [7] + objection concerning consubstantial A.

flesh, in which he accepted suffering and death in human form and
came as far as the tomb and hell, and in which he also [1] effected the
resurrection from the dead [2]. And God the Word made demonstration
of flesh and blood and soul, through his own indivisibility from the
seed of David, as it is written. For [3] what less than you does Marcion 5
say ? Does he not (posit) a body which has a heavenly appearance in
human form only and not in truth ? What else does Mani say, (if) not
a body in divine appearance in our form only, but different from human
flesh, whose nature and not activity he wickedly calls sin ? Such is
their wickedness. 10

* p. 47   **13**   Therefore it is not right for the pious to use such inventions,
but (to hold) that the Word who before ages is consubstantial with the
Father, in the end set up anew the fashioning and being of Adam from
the holy and God-bearing virgin, and made it his own by union. And
thus was revealed as a man Christ, who is God before ages. « And we 15
are the members of Christ, as it is written, from his flesh and from his
bones [4] ». So what is all this disputation of yours of inventions, that
you make definitions in human thoughts [5] beyond human understanding, saying that instead of the inner man which is in us, there was a
heavenly mind in Christ ? O lawless will and weak and unseemly words 20
of those who do not understand first this [6], that Christ is not defined in
one way, but in the name itself which is one [7] there is seen an indication of two activities, an indication of the godhead and of [8] the humanity. And [9] therefore Christ is called man and Christ is also called God ;
and Christ is both God and man, and Christ is one. 25

   So vain is your wisdom, as you try to see something else other than
Christ in himself. For those called Christs in a putative sense may
perhaps be visible by your argument. But he who is by nature and
alone the true Christ cannot be depicted by human thought, as you
dare and become presumptuous to do. Neither ⌈prophet nor apostle [10] 30
* p. 48 nor * any of the evangelists said these things which you try to utter,
in that you have become shameless in your souls [11]. For if Christ is
other than the heavenly mind which was in him, and that mind was
perfect, then there are two according to your argument. And what
you are preaching to be blasphemy, the same you are found guilty of 35

---

[1] also *om.* F. — [2] + explanation of « the Word became flesh » A. — [3] for *om.* A.
[4] *Eph., 5, 30.* — [5] thought F. — [6] + the name of Christ A. — [7] one *before*
indication *tr.* F. — [8] of *om.* A. — [9] and *om.* F. — [10] prophets nor apostles F.
[11] + objection A.

thinking. Even the prophets possessed a heavenly mind, who spoke
heavenly things and future [1] things as if they were present.

But why are you able to say these things at all, like that our inner
man is not confessed in Christ ? So why do you say of the soul, that
the body and soul are the outer man, as if one were saying blood and
flesh. But as the body and blood do not escape touch or piercing, as
they are visible, show us a soul which does not flee them, which is
visible [2]. And if you are not able to show this, the argument is clear
that the soul cannot be seen or killed by a man, like the body, as our
Lord said. So believe that our inner man is the soul, and this the first
creature shows and the second dissolution indicates. For [3] not only
are these things seen in us, but they are also visible in the very death
of Christ : the one came as far as the tomb, the other went as far as
hell. But since these places are separated by a great distance, the tomb
receives bodily coming, whither went the body, but hell (received) the
incorporeal.

14   How, when our Lord came there incorporeally, was he thought
to be a man by death ? It was in order to establish for those spirits * who   * p. 49
were held in bonds the form of his own soul, which was incapable of
receiving the bonds of death, as present to those present; in order to
break the bonds of those souls that were held in hell, when he fixed the
bounds of the resurrection; that the creator and maker of man and
(who) had cast him under punishment, the same being present should
liberate completely man by himself through his own form. For death,
despite being very powerful, had not subjected to itself the human
soul ⌐by seizing in bondage [4]; nor again had corruption violently
snatched the body and committed it to corruption, as if the actions
had been unstudied. For to have such a thought is wicked. But he
who made the inquiry [5] of disobedience and brought a double judgement of punishment, made excuse : to the earthly, saying : « Dust you
are and to dust you will return [6] », and thus corruption receives the
body, since the Lord himself decreed; but to the soul : « By death you
will die [7] », and thus man is divided into two, and to two places he was
condemned to go. Therefore he who decreed was needed, that he by
himself might loose the sentence of his judgement, having appeared
in the innocent and sinless form of one condemned, that the reconcilia-

---

[1] bountiful F.   —   [2] + that the soul cannot be killed A.   —   [3] and F.   —   [4] of
bondage A.   —   [5] enquiries A.   —   [6] *Gen.*, 3, 19.   —   [7] *Gen.*, 2, 17.

tion of God to man might take place, and the liberation of all men through a man might occur, in the newness of the image of his Son, Jesus Christ our Lord.

But if you are able to indicate yet [1] another place of condemnation, rightly then you would say that man is divided into three. From two places he was involved in the calling back from the beginning, but in the third the bound remained in bonds. But if you are unable to indicate another place apart from the tomb and hell, from which man was completely freed when Christ freed us in his form, perfect and true like ours — how do you still say that God has not yet been reconciled with humanity? So how did the Saviour come? Was it as unable to loose all men; or as abhorring the mind which had once sinned; or [2] as fearful lest he also share in sin if he were to become a perfect man, although he is God? But those who think thus are full of wickedness. For what definition do you apply to sin when you say these things [3], saying that sin is natural, like the impious Mani?

15 If you have thoughts of this kind, then you become accusers of the creator of nature. When God made Adam in the beginning, did he give him any sin springing up with his nature? So what further need was there of a commandment? How did he condemn him after he had sinned? How even before the disobedience did Adam not know good and evil? Whom God created for incorruption and as the image of his immortality, his nature he made sinless and with free-will. « But by the envy of the devil death entered the world [4] », since he found the invention of transgression. And thus from disobedience to the commandment of God, man became susceptible to the * implantation of the enemy [5]. And sin henceforth works by the will of man with regard to every desire. Not that the devil activated [6] the nature within him — far from it! — for the devil is not the creator of nature, as the wickedness of the Manichaeans [7] has it; but he worked the inclination of his will from the transgression. And thus death reigned over all men [8]. « So therefore, he says, the Son of God came to loose the works [9] of the devil [10] ». What works of the devil's did the Son of God loose? The nature which God had made sinless and the devil had turned to the

*p. 50

*p. 51

---

[1] yet *om.* F. — [2] or *om.* F. — [3] + against those who say that sin is created F (in margin, later serto hand). — [4] *Wis.*, 2, 24. — [5] + who said above, that over the good seed he cast (read ܙ̈ܝܙ܆) evil F. — [6] made A. — [7] worms (!) F. — [8] + end F (margin, later hand). — [9] work A. — [10] *1 Jn.*, 3, 8.

transgression of the commandment of God and the invention of the
death of sin, this God the Word set up in himself as insusceptible to the
devil's propensity and invention. And therefore our Lord says : « The
ruler of this world comes, and in me finds nothing [1] ». But if the ruler
5 of this world found nothing in Christ of his own deeds, much more did
Christ leave nothing of his creation to the ruler of this world [2]. Or
indeed for this reason he found nothing in him [3], because Christ showed
perfect newness in order to make complete redemption of the whole
man [4], of the rational soul and of the body, that the resurrection
10 might also be perfect.

So in vain do the Arians make a show of learning, positing that the
Saviour [5] took flesh only, wickedly attributing the idea of the passion
to the impassible [6] godhead [7]. * And in vain do you also by another   * p. 52
invention think equal thoughts [8] to theirs, and say that he used a
15 limiting form, that is [9] an instrument, and that instead of the inner
man in us there was a heavenly mind in Christ. And how was [10] he
grieved and sad and praying, and is it written : « Jesus was disturbed
in his spirit [11] » ? These are the attributes of neither mindless flesh nor
of immutable divinity, but of a soul that has understanding, that [12]
20 grieves and is disturbed and sad, and feels pain through its mind.

16 But if you do not wish to understand these things in this way,
since there are three opinions that have been adduced — phantasy and
blasphemy and the truth — which do you choose ? For by supposing
that what was said was said in supposition, the things which actually
25 took place are also considered to be phantasy. But if they were said
in truth and did take place, yet the soul of the Lord was completely [13]
different from his mind, as he has God the Word as mind, then the
immutable was changed to grief and sadness and trouble — but to
think these things is wicked. Even if the gospels say : « Jesus was
30 troubled in his spirit », yet our Lord indicates his mind by saying :
« My soul is troubled [14] ». But if our Lord indicates the mind of his soul
it is (to indicate) his (common) feeling with our soul, that in this way
we should think that suffering is also his, yet confess him to be impassible. For just as he saved us by the blood of his flesh, so also by the

35
[1] *Jn.,* 14, *30.* — [2] + which he said above concerning the fact that over the good
seed he cast evil A. — [3] it F. — [4] + both F. — [5] salvation F. — [6] impassible *om.* A. — [7] + against the passibility of the godhead A. — [8] thought A.
[9] + of F. — [10] is A. — [11] *Jn.,* 13, *21.* — [12] and F. — [13] completely
om. A. — [14] *Jn.,* 12, *27.*

And how did he give on behalf of all a substitute for salvation? Or
* p. 56 how did the hold of death receive complete dissolution, if Christ * had
not set up in himself as sinless the soul which had sinned through knowledge? So [1] according to your argument, death still reigns [2] over the
inner man. For over whom else did it ever reign except over the soul 5
which had sinned through knowledge? As it is said : « The soul which
sins will also die [3] ». For which the Lord laid down and gave his own
soul in exchange [4] for salvation [5]. Whom did God condemn from the
beginning — the creature of him who created, or the action of the
creature? If God condemned the creature of him who had created, he 10
condemned himself, and he was like men. But if it is impious to think
this of God and he condemned the action of his creature, then he
removes the action and renews the creature. « For we are his [6] work,
who have been created for good works [7] »

20   But again you say that we call God him who (was born) from 15
Mary. So how do you say, like Marcion, that God [8] came and God
intangibly came forth, yet [9] has a nature incapable of receiving human
flesh? Or how do you call him God, like Paul of Samosata? For that
is the manner of his wickedness, who confesses to be God him who (was
born) from Mary, who was determined before worlds but had the 20
beginning of his being from Mary. For he confesses the Word to be
active and that there is wisdom from heaven in him; for he attributes
(to him) more than you according to his wickedness, as you yourselves
say that there was a heavenly mind in an animate soul. For an animate body is not already a perfect man, nor a heavenly mind already 25
God. For a body is called animate, as to it the name of a soul applies
* p. 57 hypostatically. * For the body of a man is called a body and not a soul;
and the soul of a man is called a soul and not a body. They are different
with regard to each other — that is spirit to body. « But who, he says,
knows the mind of the Lord? [10] » The mind of the Lord is not yet the 30
Lord, but the Lord's will or thought or action directed to some object.

So [11] how do you find these inventions to utter, trafficking created
words against the Word of God? But the church of God has not so
received nor so handed on, but, as it is written, God the Word who is
with God from before the ages in the fulness of the ages came, and 35
was born a son of man from the holy virgin and from the holy spirit;

---

[1] so *om.* A.   —   [2] + also F.   —   [3] *Ez.*, 18, *4.*   —   [4] force A.   —   [5] + objection A.
[6] his *om.* F.   —   [7] *Eph.*, 2, *10.*   —   [8] + who F.   —   [9] yet *om.* F.   —   [10] *Rom.*,
11, *34.*   —   [11] For a fragment in S see *Appendix*, p. 107.

as it is written : « Until she gave birth to her firstborn son [1] », « that
he might be the firstborn among many brothers [2] ». And the same is
true God and the same true man, that he might suffer on our behalf
as a man, and as God save (us) from sufferings and from death. So in
5 vain do you imagine those thoughts you have, that the flesh by itself
can work renewal, as you suppose through imitation; yet you do not
think that imitation is the imitation of an action that occurred previously, otherwise it would not be called imitation. Since you confess
in Christ a renewal of the flesh only, you blaspheme in your error.
10 For if without the leader it were possible for the flesh to effect renewal
for men without Christ — for what is led follows the leader — what
need would there have been of the coming of Christ ?

     * 21   And vain are also those who say that Christ came as one of   * p. 58
the prophets. For which of the prophets, being God, also became man ?
15 Why « did the law perfect nothing [3] » ? Why did death reign also [4] over
those who had not sinned in the likeness ? Why did our Lord also say :
« If [5] the Son will free you, in truth you will be free [6] » ? Was it not
according to the renewal (effected) in him and the perfection, through
which we [7] who believe are renewed by the imitation of, and fellowship
20 in the perfect renewal ? But by you everything has been invented that
you should prepare one mind of blasphemy. And the soul in (your)
interpretation sometimes you call a mind without intelligence, sometimes actually existent sin; and sometimes you reject the flesh as the
creator of sin, sometimes as created, sometimes as heavenly, sometimes
25 as consubstantial with the Word, in order to confirm in yourselves
complete denial.

     For just as Arius lapsed from the faith and found in the ineffable
and true birth of the Son from the Father suffering and cutting off
and flow, that through wicked words he might cast the unstable into a
30 pit of lawlessness — « for the mouth of one outside the law is a deep
pit [8] »; similarly again Sabellius thought the Son to be without hypostasis and the holy Spirit to be without existence, accusing us of a
division of the Godhead and of the primacies, and of numberings [9] of
gods, sinking into a Jewish idea. Similarly Mani too, disbelieving our
35 Lord's taking flesh and becoming man, was in every way wicked,
saying that * man is subject to two creators, the bad and the good. In   * p. 59

---

[1] Mt., 1, 25. — [2] Rom., 8, 29. — [3] Heb., 7, 19. — [4] also om. A. — [5] and
if F. — [6] Jn., 8, 36. — [7] we om. F. — [8] Prov., 22, 14. — [9] a numbering F.

condemnation. But these ones imagine a change of the Word, and think to be a supposition the sufferings of the dispensation. And sometimes they say the body of Christ is uncreated and heavenly, and sometimes consubstantial with the Godhead. And again they say that instead of the inner man Christ had a heavenly mind. For, they say, 5 in the form of an instrument he used the ruling (faculty); for they do not believe that he became a complete man. For, they say, where there is a perfect man, there is sin; and there is no way for two perfects to be as one. If there is found also in Christ the contention of sin which is in us, then he too would be in need of purification like us, if that 10 which thinks and leads in us — that is the body — Christ had showed in himself when he became man. But they say he took (a body) without a mind that he might be mind for himself, and that he in no way taste sin, neither in his godhead nor in his irrational bodily aspect. For the flesh does not sin when that which leads the flesh — that is that which 15 thinks within it — has not previously considered the action of sin, and * p. 62 acted through * the body to complete the sin. So that Christ shows the body in a new way and in a likeness, but that which thinks in us in a new way through similarity, (shows) both equality and separation from sin, as each of us shows in himself; and thus Christ may be 20 deemed (to be) without sin.

3 These are their subtelties and retrograde thoughts, for there is no reason in them. For great is the error of unbelief thought up in human minds. So let us put to them the meaning and will of God : « For the Lord swore and will not repent [1] ». And let us indicate the 25 fulfilment of the dispensation, and let us posit the grace of perfect help. And let us ask them these titles, whether they agree with the predictions of the prophets, or again are in accord with the apostolic commandments; or (if) they accept the warnings of the fathers or reject [2] the explicit sayings of our Lord; so that from the predictions 30 of the prophets and from the apostolic teachings and from the things completed in action by our Lord there may take place a confession of the truth and a refutation of the error.

Say now, O inventors of these new tidings of yours — for it is not otherwise — whence did you profess to say the flesh is uncreated ? For 35 in this way you imagine the godhead of the Word to have fallen and changed into flesh, or you think the dispensation of the passion for

---

[1] *Ps.*, 109, *4.* —   [2] *Syriac* : we rejected.

death and the resurrection to be a supposition. For only the holy
Trinity has been shown to be uncreated, which exists absolutely and
eternally and immutably and unalterably. For Christ took his origin
in the flesh from men and from your brothers, as it is written; and he
5 is passible and the first-fruits from the resurrection of the dead, as
the law previously announced. How is the uncreated said * to be passi-   * p. 63
ble ? And how is the passible called uncreated ? For if you say that the
being of the uncreated Word is passibility, you blaspheme against
the Godhead. And if the passible flesh, which has bones and blood
10 and soul and all the (characteristics) of our body, fitted and united
(these) to itself and became visible and palpable, then by saying this
to be uncreated you fall in two ways. Either you suppose to be phantasy the showing forth and true sufferings, like the impious Manichaeans with whom you agree in this respect, in saying that he is
15 from the uncreated nature of the Godhead. And why do you find fault
with and blame those who dream to say that God (was) in human form
of the flesh ?

4 But you say that it became uncreated by the union with the
uncreated. And so your error is seen to be saying thus : for the union
20 of the body to God the Word took place from the womb, and thence
the Word, who came from heaven, established it; it did not previously
exist before the coming of the Word. Which is from Mary alone, who
was born from Adam and is counted in the genealogy from Abraham
and from David with Joseph her betrothed, who are both one flesh,
25 as it is written, not by intercourse with each other but as they are one.
And it is testified that they remained without intercourse. Thus
Christ was born in Bethlehem of Juda; he called Joseph « father »,
who was with Mary from Adam. And he was wrapped in swaddling-
bands and placed in a manger. And he was lifted up by Simon in the
30 temple; and he was brought to circumcision in the flesh according to
the law, and he grew in stature.

But if he was uncreated in the union, how was he not * seen to be   * p. 64
perfect ? But, (you) say, the Word wished increase of stature to take
place. For increase to be attributed to the uncreated is (a feature) of
35 the impious. For what is uncreated by nature can receive neither
completion nor deficiency, for it is joined and united to the uncreated
and is called proper to the uncreated. And it is not itself uncreated,
lest the memory of the union be blotted out, and again the help of
the love be made void, and the weakness which henceforth exists in

humanity then fall into despair, (humanity) which learns from you and
according to you, that it has no affinity with God, and again there be
obscured the gift of grace. For who hears that the body of our Lord is
uncreated, and he is confident in himself that the things which were
created he does not know, will he not understand that the scriptures 5
are found to be lying, and that he has no communion in the intimacy
of Christ? If the uncreated took an uncreated body, then the first
creation has been made void, and the prototype Adam is destroyed,
whose [1] descendants we are until today according to bodily succession.
How then did Christ make us his friends and companions? And how 10
again does the apostle say : « He who sanctifies and all who are sanctified are from one [2] »?

  5   Let no one dare and think about the divinity of the Son, that as
he is from God so are we also, which the impious Arians have the
presumption to say; but truly (let them think) this concerning the mani- 15
festation of the flesh and concerning the form of a servant — that is of
the first of creation Adam and which he who in the form of God is
God received. And this is altogether the case in creation : that which
has not yet come into being is not called created but is said * to exist.
Why then do you suppose that that which did not come into being 20
at all to be like that which came into being in the Word, and do you do
an injustice with praise of the Word, and reckon that nothing at all is
to be confessed in the uncreated? For we understand as uncreated only
the Trinity, so that to say the uncreated is passible is impious, as
also to call the passible uncreated. For the nature of a created man 25
became the Word's own by the union; but for any one to say it is
co-eternal with the nature of God and equal to the same nature — it is
very impious that any one should think that. For the Lord made
proof of the flesh [3], that it had bones and blood and had a soul that
grieved and was troubled and gloomy. And no one would say that these 30
are of the nature of godhead; for they became God the Word's own
willingly by nature, in that he submitted to human birth, that he
might raise up in himself in a new image his own creation, which had
been dissolved in sin and corruption and death. Therefore he effected
the condemnation [4] of sin on earth, and the dissolution of the curse on 35
the cross, and the cancelling of corruption within the tomb, and the

* p. 65

---

  [1] *Syriac* : where. — [2] *Heb.*, 2, *11*. — [3] For a fragment in S see *Appendix*, p.
106. — [4] *Syriac* : love.

loosing of death in hell. He ⌜passed through⌝ [1] every place to accomplish
salvation for all men, and showed in himself the image of our form.

But why was it necessary for God to endure birth from a woman, and
the maker of worlds growth in stature and the numbering of years, and
5 again the cross or tomb or hell, to which we had been made subject,
unless he was seeking us out, that he might give us life through our
own form, and call us to the form and likeness of the * perfect image?   * p. 66
For how would there have been a form with regard to perfection, unless
had first existed the flawless perfection? As the apostle said : « Put
10 off the old man and put on the new, who was created in God, in
righteousness and in holiness and in truth [2] ».

6 So whence have you learned to call the body uncreated? If
nature became uncreated by a change, well then (it would be) invisible
and immortal and also incapable of death. And how then did the Lord
15 die, if the uncreated came upon earth in an uncreated (form)? How
then did he become visible and palpable, as it is written : « We have
seen and touched with our hands [3] » ? For how do (you) say what is not
written and what is not right to think? For you are giving to all the
heretics, as (we) said from the beginning, impious thoughts, to mention
20 which is fearful. Either deny then the holy scriptures, which confess
these things, or do not have any opinion outside what is written or
say words which contain error and are incurable.

But again you say that we do not worship creation. O foolish ones!
Why do you not understand that although the body was created as the
25 Lord's own, it did not receive the worship right for a created thing?
For it became the body of the uncreated Word. For offer worship to
him whose body it became. Thus worship is its due and it should be
worshipped with divine worship. For the Word, whose body it is, is
God. For when the women approached, he prevented them and said :
30 « Do not approach me, for I have not yet ascended to my Father [4] »;
and he indicated that ascension was necessary and that ascension
was one. Nevertheless, * approaching they took hold of his feet and   * p. 67
worshipped him; they took hold of feet and worshipped God — feet
that have flesh and bones and sensation; but because they were
35 God's, they worshipped (him) as God.

And elsewhere the Lord says : « Touch me and know that a spirit

---

[1] *Syriac* : made.   —   [2] *Col., 3, 9; Eph., 4, 24.*   —   [3] *1 Jn., 1, 1.*   —   [4] *Jn.,* 20.
17.

does not have flesh and bones, as you see I have [1]». Not « I am [2]», but
« you see I have», although he is certainly a spirit. « For God is a
spirit [3]». And as he says « I have » and makes proof of it, how did he
say : « A spirit does not have flesh and bones, as you see I have»,
Not « I am », but « you see that I have ». This he taught, that the nature 5
of a spirit is something ineffable. The sensation of the body was like
ours, which he made his own from the virgin, not at the time of dispensation but by natural birth, that the body might be such naturally,
by the indivisible union with God the Word. In this way also death
occurred, the body receiving it naturally; but the Word willingly 10
endured it and freely offered his own body to death, in order that he
might suffer naturally for us and also rise for us divinely. All the
birth and business of death is seen to be for our seeking and restitution.

    7 These things are so and are confessed in the catholic church of
God. How again do you say that his body is from heaven, and why did 15
Christ make it his own ? Say ! For (was it) to bring down the body from
heaven to earth, and to make the invisible visible, and non-disgraceful

    * p. 68 capable of disgrace, and the impassible and immortal passible * and
mortal ? What use would there be in these things, O foolish ones, if you
say that what was done in Christ was what occurred in the first of 20
creation, Adam ? Unless Christ had raised up the fall of Adam incom-
parably highly, who was revealed in the form of a body of sin, and
had condemned sin in the flesh ; thus he also lived on earth in the flesh ;
and again he showed his flesh to be insusceptible of sin, which from
the beginning of creation Adam had had without sin, and from the 25
transgression of the commandment had made it susceptible of sin,
and had fallen into death and corruption. This he raises up naturally
without sin, to show that the Creator is not the cause of sin; and like
the creation of the prototype he established his own nature, that he
might be proof of being free of sin.   30

    In vain then do those who exult dream and say that the Lord's
body is from heaven [4]. Although certainly Adam brought it down
from heaven to earth, Christ took it up from earth to heaven. And
Adam brought down what was sinless and innocent to corruption and
condemnation. But Christ showed it to be incorruptible and saved 35
from death, so that he might have power on earth to forgive sins, and

---

[1] *Lk.*, 24, *39.* — [2] in margin, later hand: against Julian. — [3] *Jn.*, 4, *24.* —
[4] For a fragment in S see *Appendix*, p. 106.

show incorruptibility from the tomb, and by his entrance into hell
might loose death, and announce to all the resurrection. Because God
created man for incorruption and made him in his eternal image, but
« by the envy of the devil death entered the world [1] », and death reigned
5 over it for corruption. But he did not neglect that, he who became
man yet was not changed into the form of a man. Nor again did he
neglect * the existence of man. For he did not make an « airy » demon-   * p. 69
stration. But although he is God by nature, he became a man, that
one from two, in everything perfect, he might show a true and natural
10 birth. Therefore it is said : « And God gave him a name above all
names [2] », both that he might rule in heaven, and have power and
execute judgment.

8   For the Creator of all was revealed as a son of man : not that he
became anything different, but the second Adam, that from the name
15 we might recognise the truth. And the apostle shows the head of
creation, Adam, to be first; for he first shows the animate and then
the spiritual. But this saying « animate » and « spiritual » was not to
show different bodies but the same body : the first (with) the power
and the nature of soul, because it is animate; the second (with) the
20 power and the nature of spirit, because it is spiritual. « For God the
Word is a Spirit [3] ». For thus what is said about us is to be understood,
in that (scripture) said : « The spiritual one judges everything; but
man who is animate does not receive the things of the spirit [4] ». Certainly the body of both is one : the one is considered spiritual by partici-
25 pation in spirit; the other remains animate by the power only of the
soul, in that it is soul.

Not at all would Christ be, or be said to be, a man only as you claim,
he who brought some new thing from heaven, but to have become a
son of man. And if he became on earth a son of man, certainly he was
30 born not from the seed of man but from the holy Spirit. So one is the
first of creation, Adam, and we understand this former to be his son.
For no one else is described as the man who was in heaven, except
Adam; that he might have a body from heaven * and become the son   * p. 70
of man beside Adam. Therefore Matthew too describes him as the son
35 of Abraham and David; but Luke reckons him in the genealogy as the
son of Adam and of God. If now you are pupils of the gospel, do not
speak evil of God, but agree with what has been written and done.

---

[1] *Wis.*, 2, 24.   —   [2] *Phil.*, 2, 9.   —   [3] Cf. *Jn.*, 4, 24.   —   [4] *1 Cor.*, 2, 14-15.

But if you wish to say other things apart from what has been written, why do you fight with us who have not been persuaded to hear nor to say (anything) save what has been written? But our Lord said : « If you remain in my word, in truth you (will be) free [1] ».

9 How then will those be considered to be Christians and believers, [5] who do not agree with the things that have been written nor believe the things that have been done? But you dare to define things above nature. « Is this struggle that you are preparing for men a little thing for you? And thus again do you offer trouble to the Lord? [2] » But if those who did not believe the prophets were condemned, how much [10] more those who do not believe in our Lord? For the things that he wished and planned for the destruction of sin and death, how do you dare to say or determine other things instead? For if we confess him, he too will confess us; « and if we deny him, he too will deny us; yet if we do not believe, he will remain faithful, for it is impossible for him [15] to deny himself [3] ». Whence did you acquire this unbounded daring, that you say things that are not written and think things contrary to piety?

For you have dared to say that the flesh is consubstantial with the
* p. 71 Godhead, neither understanding * nor seeing that your impiety is for [20] you a double error. For you have thought up these things to say in order to deny the flesh and blaspheme the Godhead. « We — you say — do not confess him born of Mary to be consubstantial with the Father ». These fine words, as you suppose, are seen to be superfluous and useless. But what believer does not confess that when God the Word [25] came, he came forth as a man from the holy virgin, and is consubstantial with the Father, and became man from the seed of Abraham, whose son he was called; and although the Word is consubstantial with God, he became a son of man in the flesh from David; and therefore the prophets and apostles and evangelists reckon Christ's genealogy [30] in the flesh from the seed of David. How do you not fear when you say these things that you are proclaiming the flesh, which is reckoned in the genealogies to be from the seed of David, to be consubstantial with the Word?

Or again as (we) say, you say this irrationally, nor do you understand [35] that « consubstantial » is identity of nature without division, which exhibits in itself its own perfection. For as the Son, when he is con-

---

[1] *Jn.*, 8, 36. — [2] *Is.*, 7, 13. — [3] *2 Tim.*, 2, 12-13.

fessed to be consubstantial with the Father, is called perfect with
regard to perfect, like the holy Spirit — for he is consubstantial with
the holy Trinity — so do you also give then the flesh, in that it is
consubstantial, the same perfection with regard to the fulness of the
5 Word; and according to your argument it will be preached that there
is instead of the Trinity, a quaternity. And whence is this invention of
impiety?

10 But these ones say that the flesh became consubstantial with
the Word. How did it become consubstantial? Say! It became the
10 Word; it became the Spirit. But if, indeed, what is not by nature
godhead becomes godhead by transformation, * why then do you   * p. 72
reprove the Arians, who put forward this opinion about God the
Word? For scripture certainly says : « The word became flesh [1] »,
not : the flesh became the Word. For the Word is said to have become
15 flesh, because it was the flesh of the Word himself, not any man's.
That is, God became man. And it is said that he became flesh lest
anyone should miss the name of the flesh. But if this natural union
that God the Word had with his flesh without confusion does not
suffice for you, and that he is God and also became man, now you
20 wish neither to hear nor believe, nor are you satisfied to hear that the
body of God is above all thoughts of praises, as it is said : « He will
transform the body of our humility into the likeness of the body of
his glory [2] », which is its indication of the world to come. And again it
is called the body of his glory, as our Lord said : « When the son of
25 man will come in his glory [3] ». But the son of man, in that he became
a son of man, we confess to be Judge of the dead and living, and King
and Lord and Lord of truth.

But you wish to forget the name of the body, (and) again that Christ
is called man. And how do you read the divine scriptures? For Matthew
30 wrote « the book of the birth of Jesus Christ, son of David, son of
Abraham [4] ». And John : « In the beginning was the Word, and the
Word was with God and the Word was God [5] ». For if you wish to
examine separately the Word of God and the son of David, there
would be two * named according to your argument. But if you believe,   * p. 73
35 being instructed by the holy scriptures, that the Word is God and
also became a son of man, you will recognise that God the Christ is one :

---

[1] *Jn.*, 1, *14* — [2] *Phil.*, 3, *21.* — [3] *Mk.*, 8, *38.* — [4] *Mt.*, 1, *1.* — [5] *Jn.*,
1, *1.*

the same both God and man, that through the double-faceted preaching
of his coming the persuasiveness of his passion and his impassibility
might have good proof. As the apostle says : « The man Jesus Christ,
who gave himself for us, who is God blessed above all for ever and
ever, Amen [1] ». And he wrote to Timothy, saying : « Remember Jesus 5
Christ, who rose from the dead, from the seed of David [2] ». And he
again said : « Preach my death until he comes [3] ».

11   Thus the confession of consubstantiality denies the name of the
body and the fact that Christ is called a man. Unless indeed his death
be preached until he come, deny the scriptures. For they preach about 10
his death that by the fact that you do not confess Christ, who suffered
in the flesh, to be consubstantial with the Father and consubstantial
with the Spirit, you are saying that the divinity of the Father and of
the holy Spirit like him is susceptible of death. And you have become
more impious than the heretics. For the death of the flesh was that of 15
him who was by nature Word. For the Father did not put on the body,
nor did the holy Spirit, as those of the party of Valentinus dream in
their impiety. But « The Word became flesh [4] », and therefore we confess
Christ to be God and man. We do not say these things as if separately
— far from it — but again according to the holy scriptures, in order to 20
preach the passion and death that occurred, until he comes. We do not
confess the passion and death to be of the flesh and of the Word ; but
*p. 74 we believe the Word to be unchangeable * and immutable. Therefore it
is the same who suffered and did not suffer ; who by the nature of his
godhead is impassible and unchangeable and immutable, but suffered 25
in the flesh, as Peter says : « Christ suffered for us in the flesh [5] », and
tasted death in the flesh, and « He became mediator between God and
men, the man Jesus Christ, who gave himself as salvation on our
behalf [6] ». And again : « There is no mediator for one person, but God
is one [7] ».
                                                                              30

12   Therefore they are in error who say that the Son who suffered
is one, and another he who did not suffer. For it is no other except the
Son of God who accepted the suffering and death. But the impassible
and incorporeal Word consented to submit to human birth, and fulfilled everything in order to have something to offer on our behalf. 35
And : « He became superior to the angels [8] ». For the creator of the

---

[1] *1 Tim.*, 2, 5-6; *Rom.*, 9, 5. — [2] *2 Tim.*, 2, 8. — [3] *1 Cor.*, 11, 26. — [4] *Jn.*,
1, 14. — [5] *1 Pet.*, 4, 1. — [6] *1 Tim.*, 2, 5-6. — [7] *Gal.*, 3, 20. — [8] *Heb.*, 1, 4.

angels ⌜was not made superior ¹ to the angels, as if he were at some
time lower than them. Far from it! But this form of ours of a servant
the Word reckoned his own by a natural birth, that something better
⌜might arise ² from the birth from the first-created. And he has affinity
5 with us, as it is written : « We live the same life as the saints and are
associates of God ³ ». And the attributes of God naturally became its
own, not since the flesh is consubstantial or co-eternal with the godhead — for this is impiety — but it became his own by the natural and
undivisible union, from the seed of David and of Abraham, and from
10 Adam from whom we also are.

But if the flesh were consubstantial and co-eternal with the Word,
then on this ground creatures would be said to be co-eternal in every
respect with God, * who created everything. And how would they * p. 75
still be considered Christians who are entwined in these perversities ?
15 For what is consubstantial with the Word is impassible, and furthermore unsusceptible of death. And what is consubstantial is not susceptible of a hypostatic union but of a natural one. For the hypostatic
completely receives its properties. Then the praise and glory and
invention that is announced by you, denies the flesh that is from the
20 virgin, the Mother of God, and blasphemes the divinity. But if you thus
confess the Son to be consubstantial with the Father, and also the
holy Spirit and the flesh which suffered, why do you blame us for
saying a quaternity instead of a Trinity ; when behold you unwillingly
confess a quaternity instead of a Trinity, by saying that the flesh is
25 consubstantial with the Trinity ?

Then your faith is now vain. For you think like the impious Arians,
as you wickedly interpreted : « The Word became flesh ». For the
Word became flesh, not that the Word might no longer be Word,
but that the Word might be in the flesh. But ⁴ the Word became flesh
30 that the Word might be Word for ever, and the Word might also have
flesh ; in this he accepted both suffering and death, and in human form
would come as far as the grave and hell ; in this he also effected the
resurrection of the dead. And through the flesh and blood and soul
God the Word made demonstration, through this which he had accepted
35 indivisibly from the seed of David, as it is written. For what else more
than you does Marcion say ? Does he not say the body is a heavenly

---

¹ *Syriac* : did not remain; *corr* : was not made superior. — ² *Syriac* : but one
(sic !). — ³ *Eph., 2, 19.* — ⁴ *Syriac* : if

in bonds. But if you are unable to indicate another place beside the
tomb and hell, from these was man most completely freed. And Christ
freed us in his form, perfect and true like ours. How do you still say
that God has not yet been reconciled to our humanity ? How then did
our Saviour come ? Was it as unable to loose all men, or again as ₅
rejecting that which had once sinned — that is the mind — or again as
fearful lest he share in sin if he became a perfect man, although he is
God ? But those who suppose thus are full of impiety. What do they
say and define concerning sin, who say that sin is natural ? In this
they think like the impious Mani, and become accusers of the nature ₁₀
of the Creator.

15 When in the beginning God created Adam, did he render sin
implanted ? Then what need would there have been of the law ? And
why again did he condemn him after he had sinned ? And how again
before the disobedience did Adam not know good and evil ? Just as ₁₅
he created (him) incorruptible and as his own eternal image, he made
him by nature sinless and with free-will in his essence. « But by the
envy of the devil death entered the world ¹ », in that he invented
thoughts of transgressing the commandment. And thus from disobedience to the divine commandment man became susceptible to the ₂₀
seed of the enemy. And sin henceforth works by the will of man with
regard to every desire. The devil has not brought about the nature
within him — far from it ! — and the devil is not the creator of nature,
* p. 80 according to * the impious claims of the Manichaeans. But he brought
about the change of will through the transgression of the command- ₂₅
ment. And thus death reigned over all men. « So therefore, it is said,
the Son of God came to loose the works of Satan ² ». For what works of
Satan did the Son of God loose ? So because the devil had turned the
nature, which God had made sinless, to transgression of the law of
God and the invention of the death of sin, this the Word set up as ₃₀
insusceptible of change and that one's invention. And therefore our
Lord said : « The ruler of this world comes, and in me finds nothing ³ ».
But if the ruler of this world found nothing in Christ, all the more did
Christ leave nothing in his creation to the ruler of this world. Or indeed
for this reason he found nothing in him, save that Christ showed new ₃₅
perfection, in order to make complete perfect redemption for man, for

¹ *Wis.*, 2, 24. — ² *1 Jn.*, 3, 8. — ³ *Jn.*, 14, 30.

the rational soul, I say, and the body, that the resurrection might also be perfect.

In vain then do the Arians make a show of learning, positing that our Saviour took a body only, and impiously attributing the sense of 5 the passion to the impassible godhead. And vain is your other opinion, which you equally entertain and say, that he used a restricting form, that is an instrument; and instead of our inner man there is a heavenly mind in Christ. And how was he grieved and did he pray. « For he was disturbed in his spirit [1] », as it is written. These are the attributes of 10 neither flesh nor mind; not of immutable divinity, but of a soul that has * a mind which is grieved and disturbed and sad, and which again   * p. 81 feels pain knowingly.

16   But if you do not now wish to understand these things — since you adduce three ideas, phantasy and blasphemy and the truth — with 15 which are you pleased ? For he who supposes that what was said is delusion, then the things which took place will also be considered to be phantasy, But if they were said in truth and took place in truth, and if the soul of the Lord was completely different from his mind, as he had God the Word instead of his mind, the immutable was changed 20 to grief and sadness and trouble. But for anyone to consider these things is impiety. Even if the evangelists say : « Jesus was troubled in his spirit », yet they indicate the mind, which the Lord mentioned : « Now behold my soul is troubled [2] ». And if the Lord indicated the mind of the soul, this was for the fulfilment of support for our souls, 25 that in this way we should understand the suffering to be his, yet confess him (to have) impassibility. For just as he saved us by the blood of his flesh, so also by the mind of his soul he showed the victory (won) on our behalf. And he said : « I have conquered the world [3] », and elsewhere he says : « He who gave us victory [4] ».

30   But just as the blood is not thought to be common (blood) by those who fear God, as the unbelievers violently say, but it is salvation in truth; so also the intelligence does not cover over human weakness, but shows the nature of God. And thus Christ is said to be perfect God and perfect man. Not that the divine perfection was changed into the 35 fulness of humanity. For now that is impious. * Nor do we confess two   * p. 82 perfects in separation. That is foreign to piety. Nor by the growth of virtue and the assumption of righteousness. For far from it that this

[1] *Jn.*, 13, 21. — [2] *Jn.*, 12, 27. — [3] *Jn.*, 16, 33. — [4] *1 Cor.*, 15, 57.

* p. 85   **20** But again you claim that we say God is from Mary. But how do you call (him) God, like Marcion who said that God came forth and was revealed unentangled in a body, who has a nature insusceptible of a human body ? Or how again do you call (him) God, like Paul of Samosata ? For this is the disguise for his impiety, that he confesses ₅ to be God him who (was born) of Mary, and was determined before worlds, and had the beginning of his existence from Mary. For he confesses the Word has power and activity and wisdom from heaven — for he attributes a little more than you to him according to his impiety — as you yourselves say that there was a heavenly mind in an ₁₀ animate soul. And an animate body is not a perfect man, nor again is a heavenly mind God. But a body is called animate when the name soul is applied in the completeness of its hypostasis. But a man's body is called a body and not a soul; and a man's soul is called a soul, and is not a body. They are different with regard to each other — that is, ₁₅ spirit to body. « Who knows the mind of the Lord ? ¹ » For, he says, the mind of the Lord is not the Lord, but God's will. But the will is an action; and an action of the will is directed to some object.

How ² then do you think up these things to say — created words that pollute the Word of God ? But the church of God has not so recei- ₂₀ ved, nor again so handed on. But as it is written, God the Word, whom man does not approach, who is God from before the ages, at the end of times came and was born a son of man from the virgin Mary and from
* p. 86 the holy Spirit, * « that he might be the first-born among many brothers ³ », he who is both true God and true man, ⌐in order to suffer ⁴ ₂₅ on our behalf as a man and to save us from sufferings and from death as God. Vainly then do you dream and think that the body can by itself care for anything anew through imitation, since you do not understand that imitation is imitation of something that existed previously; otherwise, it would not be called imitation at all. But if you ₃₀ confess in Christ only a body newly (made), you err and are impious. For if without the leader of the body it were possible for renewal to exist among men, you have destroyed yourselves without Christ. For the leader is joined to the led. And what need would there be of the coming of Christ ?   ₃₅

21 Vain then are also those who say that the Lord came like one of

---

¹ *Rom.*, 11, *34*.   —   ² For a fragment in S see *Appendix*, p. 107.   —   ³ *Rom.*, 8, *29*.
⁴ *Syriac* : as he suffered.

the prophets. But which of the prophets was God and became man?
And why did the law perfect man [1]? And why did death reign also over
those who had not sinned in the likeness? Why again did our Lord
say : « If the Son frees you, in truth you will be free [2] »? Was it not
5 according to the renewal (effected) in him and according to the perfection (effected) in him, through which we who believe are renewed
by the imitation of, and fellowship in his perfection? But you are all
devising to prepare one will of blasphemy. And the soul you variously
define, sometimes calling it without mind, sometimes the substance of
10 sin. And again as the actor of sin you reject it from the body, sometimes
as uncreated and heavenly, sometimes as * consubstantial with the   * p. 87
Word, in order to confirm your denial completely.

For just as Arius lapsed from the faith, he previously devised in the
ineffable and true birth of the Son from the Father suffering and
15 division and flow, that through these impious words he might expel
and cast into a pit of wickedness those who are unstable. « For in
truth the mouth of the wicked is a deep chasm [3] ». Similarly also
Sabellius considered the Son to be without hypostasis, and the holy
Spirit again to be without existence, and he accused us of a division of
20 the Godhead and impiety and a numbering of gods, supported by the
Jewish idea. Similarly also Mani, doubting the Lord's taking flesh and
becoming man, was in everything impious, by saying that man is
subject to two creators, the bad and the good. Similarly also you
accuse us and say that we say two sons, and you consider us wor-
25 shippers of a man, and you raise an objection about sin. Not that in
this you are pious, but in order (to make) your error through wicked
invention the cause of falling, and to incline the simple away from the
faith to your words of impiety. « But the true foundation of God stands,
having this seal [4] ».

30   **22**   These things I have written, my beloved, although it was not
right to write anything else — for the gospel tradition is sufficient —
but rather because you asked about the hope we hold, and because
of those who wish to be whitewashed in their inventions, and do not
consider that he who speaks for himself speaks lies. For it is not possible
35 that human thoughts can describe the beauty of the body nor the
glory (of) Christ. * But we confess the things that were done as it is writ-   * p. 88
ten; and we worship the God who is, both for the confession and praise

[1] Cf. *Heb.*, *7, 19*. — [2] *Jn.*, *8, 36*. — [3] *Prov.*, *22, 14*. — [4] *2 Tim.*, *2, 19*.

of his mercy and the hope of our salvation; to whom be praise for ever, Amen.

End of the discourse of saint Athanasius, spoken by him concerning the holy (and) consubstantial Trinity, and concerning the incarnation of God the Word, and against Apollinarius.   5

1 And when they came to the place that is called Golgotha — which
is named the skull — they gave him vinegar to drink, mixed with gall.
5 And when he had tasted, he did not wish to drink. And they crucified
him and divided his garments. And for his garments they cast lots, in
order that what had been said through the prophet might be fulfilled :
« They divided my garments among themselves, and for my clothing
they cast lots [1] ». And there they sat and watched him [2].
10 The text that has been read comes from the gospel; and for its illu-
mination it is profitable to take refuge in the fathers, and from them
to declare its meaning. For they rightly understand more than us the
evangelists. And lest, as we go round in our argument, we linger on
them all, blessed Paul alone is sufficient for us to be our teacher for
15 the explanation of this matter. Blessed Paul himself writes to the
Hebrews that God cannot lie [3], but is truthful and does not lie. But it
is a characteristic of the nature of creatures to move and change
and be subject to diverse alterations, because it acquired the change
from non-existence to existence by the grace and mercy of its creator ;
20 and according to Paul's saying : « He who called the non-existent as
existent [4] ». But the God of all, through his Word is creator, and has
true existence unchangeably, with his Word and by his nature. And
this * he teaches through the prophet, and says : « You have seen me, * p. 90
you have seen me; that I am and do not change [5] ». And about men
25 he sings in the psalm, saying : « I said in my agitation that every man
is a liar [6] ». But concerning God Moses bears witness in the law : « God
is faithful and true [7] ».
2 But the man who has put on God, Paul, in that he was versed in
both of them, relates to us the difference of God with regard to the
30 creatures, and writes and says : « Let God be true, and every man a
liar [8] ». God is truthful, not by being not untruthful — for there is
nothing contrary to him, nor like a man is he confirmed to be truthful

---

[1] *Ps., 21, 19.* — [2] *Mt., 27, 33-36.* — [3] *Heb., 6, 18.* — [4] *Rom., 4, 17.* — [5] *Mal.,
3, 6.* — [6] *Ps., 115, 2.* — [7] *Deut., 32, 4.* — [8] *Rom., 3, 4.*

by others — but as he is the father and begetter of truth, according to
his saying : « I am the truth ¹ ». And the truth never has any love for
falsehood. So we are the truth, according to the saying of the Psalmist,
that the Lord seeks ², and untruthfulness he casts from him and makes
alien, saying : « Alien men were false to me ³ ». For the Jews were false 5
to our Saviour ; since when they professed to be keeping the law, they
did not affirm the truth, but trespassed against the giver of the law
and plotted death for him instead of grace. So justly were they rejected ;
and the death which deceitfully they had prepared for our Saviour,
they drew and brought upon themselves — like Anania and Sapphira who 10
are mentioned in *Acts* : they made a covenant with God and were false
to their promise. And this escaped the notice of the rest of the apostles,
but was clear to Peter the servant of truth. And he expelled them,
saying : « You were not untruthful to men but to God ⁴ ». And thereby
*p. 91 a great wonder was effected. And because * this was known to Peter 15
only, he made clear to all men the death that befell Anania and Sapphira, in order to bring the majority to prudence. So it is right to fear
the example of Anania and Sapphira,

    3   and to know that what we promise God does not escape his notice,
because it is no longer ours but due to God. And if we despoil any of it, 20
we do not take of our own but the things that have been assigned to
God, and we are found to be despoiling the sanctuary. The promise is
(not) ⁵ merely for gifts, but it also extends to argument and will. Nor
if anyone is poor is he deprived of will, because our great and worship-
ful mystery does not have its promise in gift but in perfect will and 25
true faith. So we have all promised, and we are servants to the debt of
the promise ; so that the virgin must necessarily give her virginity as
something that has been promised, and again the ascetic ⁶ his abstinence, and those who are married must pay temperance and love and
honour to each other. And the sum of all — we must all (keep) faith in 30
God and temperance and righteousness and steadfastness, lest the
example of Anania and Sapphira, perverse in their will, overtake us.
Therefore the apostolic saying forewarns us : « Let us pay back to
everyone his debt : to whom tax, tax ; to whom tribute, tribute ; to
whom respect, respect ; to whom honour, honour. Let us be in debt to 35
no one, except in loving each other ⁷ ». The preacher of this message

¹ *Jn.*, 14, 6 — ² *Ps.*, 30, 24. — ³ *Ps.*, 17, 45. — ⁴ *Acts*, 5, 4. — ⁵ *Syriac* :
either. — ⁶ Fem. in *Syriac* ; but « *his* abstinence ». — ⁷ *Rom.*, 13, 7-8.

did and fulfilled this. And frankly he wrote and said : « I have fought
my struggle, I have completed my course, and I have kept my faith.
And now there is kept for me the crown of justice, with which the
righteous judge will reward me [1] ». For in that he did not cheat in his
5 promises but * kept his faith and his covenant with God, he himself * p. 92
gained from God a promise that does not shake nor fall.

4   So therefore he advises us and says : « Do not lie to one another [2] »,
and : « let no lie proceed from your mouth [3] ». For he wishes us to
become his imitators, by writing and saying : « I tell the truth and
10 do not lie [4] ». For what our Lord said is also a saying of the gospel :
« Let your word be yes, yes and no, no [5] ». For let the word of those
who are in Christ be affirmed as far as « yes » and let them not resort to
anything else or to oaths. Because it is not right for the sake of corruptible things to deride God and to take his name in oaths, especially
15 as Moses decrees : « Do not take the name of the Lord your God in
vain [6] ». For if it is at all credible to you that the name of God is
worthy of belief, all the more should it be believed before oaths. Who
is worthy to be trusted with regard to the greater, is much more
worthy of belief in regard to the lesser. But if he is not trustworthy
20 without oaths, neither is he trustworthy in taking the name of the
Lord. For how at all does he who swears bring God to witness, since
he has no faith in him, for which alone God has regard ? *Wisdom* bears
witness to this and says : « The holy spirit flees from the instruction of
deceit and shuns ignorant thoughts, and does not dwell in a body that
25 is in debt to sin [7] ».

Therefore our Lord Jesus Christ from those who invoke him first
demands faith, as he said to the blind man : « Do you believe that I am
able to do this for you [8] » ? And to him who had a lunatic demon * he * p. 93
said : « If you believe, this will happen to you [9] ». This our Saviour did,
30 not that he was in need of help from others — for he is Lord and giver
of faith — but lest he appear to be giving to people but yielding to
those who believe; and lest, furthermore, they receive help without
faith and by their unbelief lose it. But he wishes that when he bestows
grace it should remain, and that when he heals his healing should be
35 unshakeable and unfalling. He warned the paralytic and said : « Be-

---

[1] *2 Tim.*, 4, 7-8. — [2] *Col.*, 3, 9. — [3] *Eph.*, 4, 29. — [4] *1 Tim.*, 2, 7. —
[5] *Mt.*. 5, 37. — [6] *Ex.*, 20, 7. — [7] *Wis.*, 1, 4, 5. — [8] *Mt.*, 9, 28. — [9] Confusion of *Mt.*, 17, *14*ff and *Mk.*, 11, 23.

hold, you are healthy ; sin no more, lest anything evil happen to you [1] ». For as when a skilled doctor enters a patient's presence and learns from him whether he wishes to be healed, lest when he is diligent and concerned for the patient the latter be found unwilling and the doctor's cure be profitless through the opposition of the patient's will to the 5 doctor's art ; so also our Lord enquired of those whom he healed, and to those who believed he granted the grace of faith, that grace might remain with them. Now the proof of the soul's will is faith.

5   So how do those [2] who have neither faith nor truth call God as witness ? But the Spirit bears witness and says in the psalms : « The 10 Lord is near to all who call on him in truth [3] », by which only can we call on God. Not as some swear by God, who have no faith even in the least matters. Especially as the testimony of oaths gives no indication concerning affairs. For men swear not * to tarry in affairs but to establish and confirm the truth that they are not lying in what they say. But if 15 he who swears has truth and faith, what use is there in an oath ? But if there is no faith in him, why are they so impious in human and mortal affairs, calling as witness him who is above men ? For if it is not right to call to witness an earthly king, insignificant and external, in that he is superior to the judge and his summoner, why do we summon the 20 Uncreated to task and cause God himself to be judged by men ? Desist from that ! For it surpasses the greatest impiety and presumption. What then should be done ? Nothing more than that our word should be yes, yes and no, no ; and that we should not lie et all. And thus we will be seen to be truthful and imitating the true God.   25

6   But perhaps someone will object to this and say : If it is forbidden to men (to take) oaths, he who does not swear is not imitating God, because we see in the divine scriptures God himself swearing an oath. For he both swore to Abraham according to the testimony of Moses, and it is also written in *Songs* : « The Lord swore and will not repent. 30 You are priest for ever in the order of Melchisedek [4] ». And if these (quotations) are in opposition to what has been said, then men would quickly thereby trouble themselves with oaths. But this is not so, not at all ; nor let any one think of it in this fashion. For how is he who is Lord and creator of all thought of in this ? But if it is right to tell 35 the truth, his word is an oath for the instruction of those who hear him, and he enables every one to believe that what he said and

* p. 94

[1] *Jn.*, 5, 14. — [2] *Syriac* : we. — [2] *Ps.*, 144, 18. — [4] *Ps.*, 109, 4.

promised will truly occur. * God does not swear as a man, but in lieu of * p. 95
an oath we have his word. Because when God speaks with men he is
said to swear; and this is very human. When men speak they too are
found by their speaking to be trustworthy, that we might believe
5 that what God is speaking is in lieu of an oath. And as an oath confirms
the word of a man, so also what God says is considered in lieu of an
oath because of his firm and true will.

For there bears witness to this saying the oath which is written :
« The Lord, (scripture) says, swore and will not repent», since the
10 unrepentance of whatever will take place occurs by a promise in lieu
of an oath. This the Lord also shows in *Genesis* when he says : « I swore
by myself [1] ». And this is not an oath, for he does not swear by anyone
— which is the characteristic of an oath — but by himself, which
evades the suspicion of an oath. And thereby he indicates the confir-
15 mation of the promise, which all hearers must believe. Let there be
witness to this the psalmist David, in that he recalls that God swore,
in psalm eighty-eight, saying : « Where are your former blessings, Lord,
which you swore to David in truth [2] » ? God does not swear by truth, but
what he confirms he says will be in lieu of an oath for men. God swears
20 in a human fashion for belief, and it is not right from this for us to
trouble ourselves with an oath. But thus let us speak and act, our
hearers not needing an oath, but let (our) words and deeds have their
testimony in themselves. And in this way we shall imitate God.

* **7** But perhaps someone may bring as objection against us what * p. 96
25 (was done) to the Ninevites. If the word of God is an oath in that he is
true in what he says and does not lie, how did he say : « Behold within
three days Nineveh will be overturned [3] », and this saying was not
fulfilled ? And this seems to be in conflict with the previous arguments.
But God does not lie. Far from it ! Nor does his word remain without
30 fulfilment. For in his mercy he blunted his anger, and he regarded the
penitence of the Ninevites rather than their wickedness. Because the
right hand of the Highest is quick to move, as it is written : « It has
persuasive repentance [4] ». And again the word of God is not such that
after three days Nineveh would be overturned, but « for three days
35 I shall endure you, that by the long-suffering of three days you have
power to choose for yourselves repentance or anger ». And what does
the prophet say ? « Behold in three days Nineveh will be overturned ».

[1] *Gen.*, 22, 16. — [2] *Ps.*, 88, 50. — [3] *Jonah*, 3, 4. — [4] *Jonah*, 3, 9, 10?

He did not say that after three days it would be overturned; otherwise
thus it would truly have happened. For he said : « Up to three days
it will be overturned ». For this « up to three days » we are to understand as the long-suffering of God. Whereas « it will be overturned »
after the long-suffering indicates the anger that will come upon them 5
unless they repent.

And if it is not in this fashion, and because of repentance he endured
them for those three days, who restrained [1] God from immediately
destroying Nineveh ? Was it insufficient strength ? Banish the thought
and let it not enter our mind. For God is the Lord of hosts and strong 10
and mighty and long-suffering. But ignorance of their activity, you
say ? Do not suggest that either, for he knows everthing before it
* p. 97 occurs. So what * remains for us to understand (by this), except the
long-suffering and mercy and lavish love of the good Lord ? This too
the prophet knew, yet he fled, being sent in the beginning, and after 15
he had apologised the second time he said : « O Lord, are these not my
words when I was in my land ? Therefore I made haste to flee to Tar-
shish, because I knew that you are merciful and compassionate, and
long-suffering and very graceful, and forgiving towards the evil of
men [2] ».   20

Jonah fled, but not contending against God; and again he was
grieved, but not rejoicing in the destruction of the Ninevites. But this
he did, being concerned for the Ninevites. And he was fearful lest the
prophecy (made) to them be considered untrue and they begin to have
doubts and no longer receive a prophet, in that the word of prophecy 25
was despised among them. Therefore he was grieved and sad lest he
be not known, and there be revealed to the Ninevites that which was
said by his Lord : that the prophet did not lie but by divine mercy the
Ninevites were forgiven. And it was right that this saying « up to three
(days) » should have the indication of God's longsuffering. And this is 30
the custom of divine scripture : when God wishes to show his long-
suffering he indicates the limit through the expression « still ». This he
shows through Isaiah, and says : « What did I have to do to my vineyard
and did not do [3] » ? And through Jeremiah he proclaims the same :
« Again I shall strive with you, says the Lord [4] ». By saying « again », 35
he indicates his grace and his long-suffering. And he said : « Pass the

---

[1] Syriac : henceforth. — [2] Jonah, 4, 2. — [3] Is., 5, 4. — [4] Jer., 2, 9.

islands of Chettim ... [1] and realise that I am long-suffering and very graceful [2] ». And unless he had wished to be long-suffering he would not have offered advice that they should pass * the islands and learn   * p. 98 from their opponents the distinction with regard to the good. But when he did not wish to be long-suffering, but their working of evil called forth his anger, he indicated in short by saying : « No longer will I endure your sins [3] », that by this phrase « no longer » there be left nothing to explain. And he indicates his long-suffering that was made clear with regard to the Ninevites.

For it was possible for God not to be truthful ... [4] and especially by being willing. Therefore he promised Abraham ... [5]; he did not lie and granted him a son. And again he led the people out from the land of Egypt through the blessed Moses. And again to Isaac he affirmed the promise, and made him father of the two peoples. And to Jacob he promised that he would show him Joseph. And to the faithful Moses he gave faith in the things which happened to Pharaoh. And to David he promised, and gave him his promise through Solomon his son — I mean the building of the temple.

8 Why do I need to speak at length ? For there is nothing that God says which remains uncompleted. And even if someone in faint-heartedness were to seek immediately the fulfilment of the saying, yet in time the gift of the promise occurs and undoubtedly the completion of the promise in time is effected. And behold the things that a long time ago were said, in the gospel we see completed. Isaiah prophesied that from a woman unacquainted with marriage Emmanuel would be born; and he was born from the virgin Mary, and appeared as God and fulfilled the saying of the prophet. And again Micah previously announced concerning the place in which the Messiah would be born; and the Lord was revealed in Bethlehem in a manger, and he showed the prophet to be true. Zechariah proclaimed to Jerusalem the word of our Saviour; and the Lord sent and brought a foal * and rode on it, and entered   * p. 99 Jerusalem and fulfilled the prophecy. And in short, not to mention each single one by name of the things that had been written and inscribed, Christ was the summing-up of the law and the prophets. For the things that through them had been foretold and announced, he by his presence fulfilled and completed. And he said : « He who

---

[1] 6 or 7 letters blurred. — [2] *Jer.*, 2, *10*. — [3] Cf. *Jer.*, 51, *22*. (*LXX*). — [4] 10 or 12 letters blurred. — [5] 6 or 7 letters blurred.

* p. 102 sible for them to change (their minds), * but it was impossible for the prophet to lie, because he foresaw the truth. And it was impossible for him to make a mistake in this. For he saw in no other way than how it happened; and they were seen to be unbelieving. And thus was also accomplished the miracle concerning the virgin, and the wonder ₅ concerning Jonah occurred. For not because they were written, for this reason did it come into effect. But because they happened, they were foretold.

And thus also concerning the present dividing of the garments did it occur; as it happened, so it was foreseen; and it was accomplished ₁₀ as it was predicted and announced. It is written thus : « When they had crucified him, they cast lots for his garments, that what is said in the prophet might be fulfilled : They divided my garments among themselves, and for my clothing they cast lots ¹ ». And Matthew with the rest of the evangelists said truly 'division'. But John also mentioned ₁₅ the amount of the division, and narrates the cause of the lot that they threw, saying : And the soldiers, when they had crucified Jesus, took his garments and divided them into four parts. And for each one of the soldiers (there was) one part ». And he said concerning his tunic, which was without a seam : « It was woven as a whole, from above. And ₂₀ they said among themselves : Let us not tear it, but let us cast lots for it, whose it shall be; that the prophecy might be fulfilled which said : They divided my garments among them, and for my clothing they cast lots ² ».

11 But perhaps when one sees the Lord crucified and insulted and ₂₅ seized and smitten, he will be ashamed at it; seeing the King of all and wonderful Saviour being judged by Pilate and crucified by the Jews, he will lower his gaze to look down. For not even the sun endured to see this sight, and it was entirely darkened and obscured the eyes of
* p. 103 many * and restrained them from seeing; and it disregarded the law of ₃₀ shining on men and even dared to transgress it, because it saw its Lord who had commanded it to shine suffering at the hands of men. But if we enquire the cause and learn why he suffered, we shall not be ashamed but we shall wonder at his grace and mercy towards us; and we shall boast like Paul in his cross, because the Lord did not suffer ₃₅ for his own sake, but we are they who suffered in him.

---

¹ Cf. *Mt.*, 27, *35*; *Mk.*, 15, *24*; *Lk.*, 23, *34*; *Jn.*, 19, *24*; *Ps.*, 21, *19*. — ² *Jn.*, 19. *23-24.*

For the sin of men was boundlessly great, and the whole of creation was held in the grip of this evil. For it was gradually increasing and was measureless among men. And death again was reigning over all men and in all men. But our Lord is immortal and incorruptible, and
5 furthermore good and benevolent. For of the good Father he is the Word of truth and grace, who did not neglect our race when it was perishing, nor endure to see another lord hold the creation that had been created by himself. But when he saw the evil was exceedingly strong, and the mortal race unable to withstand death, nor able to
10 pay the punishment appropriate for the evil — for the greatness of the evil has surpassed every punishment — the Son again saw the goodness of the Father, and he saw that he sufficed for this, in that « Christ is the power and wisdom of God [1] ». And he was moved by his mercy, and pitied our weakness and put it on, being compassionate, according to
15 the saying of the prophet : « He bore our misfortunes and endured our weakness [2] ». And he had mercy on our mortality, which he too had put on. For Paul says : « He humbled himself as far as death, the death of the cross [3] ».

* But he also saw that we were unable to pay the punishment of * p. 104
20 death, and this he also took up. « Christ, he says, became a curse for us [4] ». And thus he assumed all our human characteristics and robed himself in our (clothes) for our sake. And he brought us near to the Father, in order that as he suffered, he might set up man unharmed by his suffering, and change small things into great ones. For he descended
25 in order to establish a way up for us ; and he accepted the experenice of birth, that we through him might reconcile the angry one. He was weakened for our sake, that we might stand in strength, and say like Paul : « I can do everything in Jesus Christ who strengthens me [5] ». He took a corruptible body, that this corruptible might put on incor-
30 ruption. He put on this mortal, that this mortal might put on immortality. And he became a perfect man and died, that we who die like men might become deified, and death no longer reign over us. For death no longer has power over him, as the apostolic saying announces. Therefore is he also crucified, to redeem us from the curse, and that
35 we might inherit blessing. For when he suffered, he was in no way hurt, but he rather gave greater blessings ; and when he died, he did not

---

[1] *1 Cor., 1, 24.* — [2] *Is., 53, 4.* — [3] *Phil., 2, 8.* — [4] *Gal., 3, 13.* — [5] *Phil., 4, 13.*

said : « I am innocent of this blood [1] », although later because of love
for the Jews, he was overcome and ran and agreed and handed him over
to the cross. Our Saviour was handed over; and when he was handed
over he was not afraid of death, but rather he was bravely prepared for
it. And he pursued the fleeing serpent. For our Saviour did not die in 5
order to remain in death, but thereby to pursue death.

14 But because wretched Satan saw the miracle effected in the
governor Pilate — that it was rather he who was judged than the one
judged by him — and his plots and arguments unavailing — as in the
beginning he tempted him on the mountain to learn if he were the Son 10
of God — he was ashamed and ineffective and kept this for the time of
death; and thought that just as he had enslaved and subdued all men,
so also he would test our Saviour in death. It is written in Luke :
« When the devil had finished all his temptations, he left him for a
* p. 108 time [2] ». That time is when the adversary realised and perceived * that 15
he would be trampled by everyone and that this hold would fail; and
this alone eluded him, because he was stripped of all, to learn if he
was our Saviour, lest when he had learned this he dare to approach the
divine power, which man cannot approach.

But our Lord, when he knew his wicked cunning, that he was 20
caring not for his own sake but for the subjection and servitude of men,
concealed and hid his divinity because of the former's thorough
insolence; and he acted like a man, lest he depart without approaching
the impassible God, but still begin to be mocked by man. And as a
man might see his enemy weakened and fearful and fleeing, and him- 25
self put on the appearance of weakness in order to summon the fugitive;
seeing the appearance of weakness thereby he will take heart to come
near him. And then the cunning enemy will lay aside the appearance
of him weakness whereby he summoned his oponent, and thus by his
invincible strength overcome his enemy. In the same way our Saviour 30
also put on human weakness for the provocation of his adversary, and
by his divine power strengthened the man against his enemy. Therefore also at the beginning of (his) death he was distressed and saddened,
and showed himself grievous unto death, and urged the Father to
cause the cup of death to pass from him; and he called out to the 35
Father : « The spirit is ready but the body is weak [3] », that when our

---

[1] Mt., 27, 24. — [2] Lk., 4, 13. — [3] Mt., 26, 41; Mk., 14, 38.

enemy Satan, who goes around as a lion to devour man, approached
him as a man, he might test the divine power.

15 And the trick that the wretch played on man happened to him
when he approached our Saviour. When he saw his bravery he was
5 afraid; but seeing the weakness 'of the body he took heart and * had * p. 109
audacity. And one could see Satan with all his hosts and principalities
and powers in flight, and on the other hand our Saviour with his
mighty and human weapons pursuing the whole company of the devil.
And there was no great interval before he despoiled the whole army of
10 the enemy. And thenceforth Satan moved all men against our Saviour;
the Jews (to) prepare to crucify him, the governor to condemn him, the
soldiers to insult him. And it was unknown to him that this was against
himself. For wickedness is blind and evil fights against itself, though
doing this unwillingly.

15 And as a man might seize a snake in his hand and wish to throw
it at another, but is himself first bitten by it; or again, he who takes
fire in his hand and wishes to harm his enemy, is himself first burned
by it — likewise also this evil makes war against those who hold it and
rather overcomes them, than those against whom it is sent. So too
20 Pharaoh, wishing to seize, was held; and when he began to pursue,
was pursued; and wishing to despoil, was despoiled; and desiring to
kill, drowned in the abyss of water. In the same way it also happened
to the devil. When he wished to tempt, he was tested; he moved the
soldiers, but it was against himself; when he was diligent at murder,
25 he brought defeat upon himself. And now when he was despoiling, the
victory was unknown to men; but despite his will the wretch brought
it into the open. And when they stripped our Saviour, and it occurred
secretly, the victory over the devil came into the open. And immediately they put on him the purple, according to the saying of John — but
30 according to the saying of Matthew and of Mark, the robe of scarlet —
and they put a crown of thorns on his head; and they stretched out
and placed a reed in his hand, and they genuflected before him in
mockery.

*16 It is a new and wonderful miracle and proof of a great victory, * p. 110
35 that they should judge him as a man, but by his death and resurrection
they should know him to be God. And whom they derided as mean and
common, him they confess as king. And in that they stripped him of
clothes of no value, they dressed him in purple. And whom they despised
in their ignorance, him they called « prophet », although unwillingly.

And whom they struck and buffeted, to him they gave the victory, a
crown and robe of scarlet and reed. Even if they did these things to
mock and insult him, yet unwillingly and unknowingly the despoiling
prevailed against themselves. But because the whole earth was dyed
with the blood of sin by the devil more than the water upon it, through 5
the fact that from the beginning it had opened (its) mouth for the
blood of Abel the just, and thereafter blood upon blood of men had
been poured out and added, as it is written : « Cursing and theft and
fornication were poured out over the earth, and blood mixed with
blood [1] », therefore the earth was cursed, as God said : « Cursed is the 10
earth which opened its mouth and received the blood of Abel your
brother [2] ». But it was also previously cursed because of Adam's
transgression : « In distress you will eat it all the days of your life ;
thorns and thistles it will bring forth for you [3] ». Henceforth it was all
full of blood, and everywhere thorns flourished because of the curse. 15
And he who had the autograph of the debt was rebellious against
everything and overweening against everyone, in that he had all men
in subjection under his hand.

Therefore when our Saviour despoiled him of these, to make a
* p. 111 remedy for men, it was not haphazardly that this happened, * but it 20
was done for the salvation of men. He received the garments in the
scarlet robe ; the thorns in the crown ; the autograph in the reed which
they made him hold, in which the devil had written against us, (that)
these too with death might have a remedy and be removed from us, and
that he purify all creation from them, and grant us instead of thorns 25
the wood of life, and that instead of the blood of sin by his pure blood
he might purify us and the whole earth, and in place of the curse give
blessings to those upon it : « Blessed are the humble, for they will
inherit the earth [4] ». Therefore he bore the blood of us all and poured
out his own blood for us, that instead of thorns he might make the 30
blessings of life to blossom for us on earth — on which the prophet
gazed and said : « I shall look on the blessings of the Lord in the land
of the living [5] ».

17 And especially he shows us the crown which he wore that he
might extirpate from us our wordly care. But the enemy unwillingly 35
treated us so that he threw our care upon himself, that when our
Saviour bore it He might make us without care with regard to our

---

[1] *Hos.*, 4, 2. — [2] *Gen.*, 4, 11. — [3] *Gen.*, 3, 17-18. — [4] *Mt.*, 5, 5. — [5] *Ps.*,
26, 13.

enemy. But the seed of the saying is freed from thorns, and by his prayer he freed us from pains and troubles. But he for our sake endured pain, and took care that we might be preserved without pains and care. Therefore our Saviour accepted the reed from them; and Satan
5 held it out to him and did not know that he was sharpening an iron weapon against himself. It is said that the reed is a destroyer of serpents. And with it he pursued the evil serpent. And according to the saying of Isaiah : « The Lord of Sabaoth pursued this evil and perverse serpent [1] », who is the devil, from whom he received the reed, his
10 destroyer; that when he was weakened the Jews also might be weakened by it, and those who believe in our Saviour might be strengthened. Similarly acted * also blessed David against Goliath,   * p. 112
who took the sword of his enemy and with it cut off his head. This too our Saviour did when he received the reed from him, not only to free
15 us from the deceit of the snake, but also to kill him and show him to be dead by the reed which he held in his hand.

Thus the wretch was mocked, and he saw that he had fallen from the things he had prepared against us, and that he was cast out and rejected from the earth, in that it was purified from blood and thorns. And he
20 saw that he had lost the autograph — that is the reed — on which he had written the debt of sin. And again he had boldness that exceeded all effrontery, but rather thereby smote himself. And this same wicked one heard our Saviour saying : « The spirit is ready, but the body is weak [2] », and he supposed that even the Word was weak with the
25 body. But the body was strengthened by the power of the Word. And again he had impious audacity, and sharpened the people in presumption against our Saviour. But he was crowned with the things of thorns. And the opposite happened to him. When he thought he had acquired what he did not have, he lost what he did have; and he re-
30 ceived nothing because our Saviour took the curse and bore it, and with it the thorns that (derived) from it. And he put on the purple robe, that the enemy might no longer be strong against us, in that he had been reproved for his wickedness by our Saviour. Now the devil in the form of thorns with his goads strikes and kicks us. But it is
35 said and likened to the purple clothing : « Just as clothing fallen in blood is not pure, so neither you are pure, because you have destroyed my land and killed my people ».

[1] *Is., 27, 1.* — [2] *Mt., 26, 41; Mk., 14, 38.*

*p. 113   * **18** Therefore now also he moved the people of the Jews and like thorns struck with his goads, but rather he himself was struck. But not thus did he stir up victory against our Saviour, like the defeat into which he fell. And they were armed against him. But when they took the reed against our Saviour, by which they beat him, immediately ₅ they were blinded and fell on each other and beat each other. Like the nations which went down against Jerusalem and which destroyed each other in the valley of Josaphat; and when they pursued Israel and came up to the bank of the river, they were entangled together and seized each other. In the same way too, those who pursued our ₁₀ Saviour struck each other unknowingly, causing him no harm but rather being hurt themselves. And just as one who wishes to cut a stone with his hand, does not cut the stone but rather hurts his hand — in just the same way those who dared to assault our Saviour, as assailing the incorruptible were themselves destroyed; and as they ₁₅ presumed against the immortal, they themselves died.

And the most grievous thing — by his own member the evil one was struck, and this to his complete shame. If he had been smitten by our Saviour, he would have been able to boast. But now by those who are subject to him and are intent on his service — by these he was ₂₀ struck. And this sufficed for his shame. But their blow did not kill the serpent. Nor was man able to do this —· a blow from them would not have hurt him — but he received a blow from the hand of our Saviour in which he held the destroying reed. Our Saviour very fittingly used a
*p. 114 human form, who took upon himself the crown of thorns, * and as a ₂₅ man permitted himself to be buffeted. And thereby the evil one was struck, that as once he had boasted to be God and had boasted again that he had tempted our Saviour, so by the murderers he might be struck and insulted and increase (his) complete shame.

19 This happened to him against his will, as he designed. He ₃₀ worked among those who were crying out against our Saviour; yet the wretch did not know that he was bringing silence upon himself. For he incited Pilate to murder; yet he did not know that instead of the fear of death he was preparing courage. He stirred up buffeting against our Saviour; yet he was unaware that thereby he was increasing ₃₅ long-suffering. And finally, he was exceedingly impious, for he did not see the virtue that was being equipped against evil. For he rejoices in evil; and every kind of evil is the weapon of the devil. And fear lest they die makes many to sin. Thus our Saviour endured all these

things to give (us) courage instead of fear, long-suffering instead of
shame, humility instead of anger. And in all these he taught virtue to
oppose evil. First he teaches and says : « To him who strikes you on
the cheek, turn also the other [1] », and : « Do not fear those who kill
5 the body [2] », and : « Do not claim back from him who takes what is
yours [3] », and : « Bless those who persecute you [4] ».

But to prevent it being thought by some people that the law and
commandment are impossible, our Saviour permitted these things to
be done to him. And by suffering he instructed all men, that when
10 anyone is insulted not to retaliate; and when anyone is mocked not to
be angered; and when anyone * is beaten, not to strike back; and not to   * p. 115
claim back from whomever takes what is yours; and altogether, not
to fear death but to despise it by the hope of future blessings. And
thus the victory over the devil and over sin will be effected more
15 easily and simply, rather than when we are beaten we strike back, and
when we are killed we kill; and we avenge our insult and murder on
our insulters and murderers. Then we foster and increase evil against
ourselves and not against our enemies; but we harm ourselves with the
punishment of evil. And judgment is reserved for those who use these
20 methods. But when like our Saviour we endure the evil-doings perpet-
rated upon us, then we must oppose our accusers with longsuffering,
and defeat those who threaten us with fortitude; and the sum of all
these — conquer death with the hope of immortality. That when the
enemy sees us he may be distressed by these things, because he has
25 fallen by such armour as Paul armed us with, saying : « Let us put on
the armour of God, that by it we may be able to resist the stratagems
of the devil [5] ». And when our Saviour endured suffering occurred the
(event) : « I saw Satan falling from heaven like lightning [6] ».

20 And immediately thereafter, after the good which had been
30 done and the fall of the enemy, they put upon him his cross, as truly
it is a sign of victory, though they did it against themselves. While
the murderous enemy was standing, they held the cross; but when he
had fallen and been overthrown, then our Saviour received the victory.
And he bore his cross, because it was right for the victor to reveal
35 openly his victory over the devil and not allow it to be otherwise save
that he himself bear his victory. He received with his victory from

---

[1] *Lk.*, 6, *29.* — [2] *Mt.*, 10, *28.* — [3] *Lk.*, 6, *30.* — [4] *Rom.*, 12, *14*; cf. *Mt.*, 5, *44*;
Lk., 6, *28.* — [5] *Eph.*, 6, *11.* — [6] *Lk.*, 10, *18.*

them also his garments as he was being led to death, that he should
put them off with death. And they were taking him hastily and leading
*p. 116 *him to the cross. And according to John's saying, he bore his own cross;
but according to the account of the rest of the evangelists, a man bore
it whose name was Simon of Cyrene. But this is not contrary to John, 5
nor did John compose the opposite of these, but both things occurred
together. Both our Saviour bore his cross and Simon again identically
bore it. Our Saviour first bore it, as victory over the devil, and willingly
and not by force did he come to the death of the cross. And Simon also
bore it, that it might be known and revealed to all men that our 10
Saviour was not dying his own death, but our death.

These things were so done, and he came urgently and hastily to
death, where he had to go up onto the cross, that on his cross he might
fix the autograph against sin which he had received from the enemy.
When he spoiled principalities and powers, he freely revealed them and 15
put them to shame by his cross. And he showed again the man whom
he had snatched from the lion's mouth, and through whose blood he
had sprinkled and purified the earth. When he was ready to do this,
he put off his garments, because, when leading the man into paradise,
he had to put off from him the clothes which Adam had put on when 20
he left paradise. When he had sinned and was about to die, he took
clothes of skin made from mortal animals, and put them on [1] — which
were a sign of the mortality which befell us through sin.

21   But our Saviour, who accepted all our (characteristics) for our
sake, put them on in order to put them off, and to dress us instead 25
with life and incorruption. He put on with them also the seamless
*p. 117 tunic that was woven as one piece from the top down, * that thereby the
Jews might be able to believe who and whence was he who put them
on : that not from the earth but from above had come the Word; and
(that) he is not divided but undivided from the Father; and although 30
he became man, he does not have a body compounded from man and
woman, but from a virgin only, woven by the art of the Spirit. So when
the murderers were dividing his clothes — for these were divisible —
they divided them into four parts; and on behalf of the four parts of
the whole world, the East and West, and North and South, he put 35
them on. And John regarded him as he put them on, and said : « Behold
the lamb of God, who takes away the sin of the world [2] ». Only the

---

[1] *Syriac* : he (God ?) put them on him (Adam ?).   —   [2] *Jn.*, 1, *29*.

tunic they were unable to divide, from fear of the miracles that were revealed by it. And this was not their own work, but that of our Saviour who was crucified. When he hung on the cross, he pursued Satan and his hosts, and frightened the murderers from dividing his
5 tunic; (that) as this remained without rent, it might be a rebuker to the Jews — which it was not slow to be, in that the veil was rent, but the tunic of our Saviour remained without division. It was not even torn by the murderers, but was preserved complete and entire. And the gospel remains in its entirety and fulness, more than the divisible
10 shadows.

Nevertheless, putting off his garments, he hastened to come to death. And when the devil saw our Saviour's ready will, and saw that he himself had fallen from heaven and had been expelled from earth, and that he had no-one to bind, but everything was full of confusion
15 for him — he was unable to remain yet frightened to flee. Nevertheless he had the thought * that those who die return to the earth, as it is   * p. 118 written : « Dust you are, and to dust you will return [1] ». And he was frightened to remain on earth, lest he seize him. Then he proceeded to ascend into the air, (that) perchance (when) for this reason the
20 Lord's body had been buried in the earth, he might keep the air clear. And in this he showed again philanthropy — that he did not die on earth, but was raised up into the air through the cross, that there he might pursue the evil snake, and drive out from there the head and ruler of the air, and apprehend there the evil spirits. Not even thus did
25 he leave the earth without healing, but when he was crucified he purified the air by the stretching out of his hands, and the earth he saved and washed through the blood from his side.

22 What then should the enemy have done, to whom all these things occurred - who was expelled from the air, chased from the
30 earth, fell from heaven, and was shamed by these things; who had promised to accomplish great things and accomplished nothing, but was overcome in everything and failed in his stratagems ? He knew that he retained hell, because this place alone remained; yet he was afraid that the Saviour would seize him even there, and chase him
35 from there and free all those who were in subjection under his hands. Therefore he moved everything and howled everywhere, wishing to bring everyone to his assistance. He incited the murderers and urged

---

[1] *Gen., 3, 19.*

them to insult the Saviour and to mock him and to deride him. And altogether he armed them with whatever was left to him; and these arrows he loosed at our Saviour, that perchance he might make him [1] subject to much sin. For the Jews were mocking our Saviour and saying : « If you are the Son of God, come down from the cross [2] ». But ₅ * p. 119 our Saviour, who is truly * the Son of God, did not wish to show that he was Son by coming down and fleeing but by remaining, and through his endurance to trample on and loose death, because he is life. He was able to come down from the cross — he who raised the other dead — but his descent would have seemed flight from death. But his ₁₀ remaining showed him who remained to be nothing other than life.

Therefore the devil was very anxious to taunt our Saviour, because he greatly wanted him to come down from the cross, and not to be among the dead and be loosed impassible [3] (in death), that he might be ruler over the dead. For he was afraid, as it is written, « lest he ascend to ₁₅ the height of the cross and take captivity captive, and take gifts to men [4] ». For he was in doubt and suspicious that this was he about whom it had been written. So again he urged all the more this stratagem on the Pharisees, that they should promise to believe in him if he were to come down from the cross. And he gave them all this advice only to ₂₀ prevent him from being among the dead and descending to hell. He again made the Pharisees say : « He saved others, himself he will not save. If he is the king of Israel, let him now come down from the cross, and we will believe in him [5] ». He did not want the Pharisees to believe in him, the serpent the teacher of unbelief, but he prayed that our ₂₅ Saviour should flee from death. Nor did he wish to learn if he could save himself, but that there should not be salvation for others. If indeed he knew that he would save others, there would have been no doubt in this, that he who saves others and grants life is himself truly Saviour and Life-giver.   ₃₀

23 So not for this reason did he abuse him, save to prevent salvation * p. 120 being effected for many. For * he who is concerned with evil knew that our Saviour would not die, but that his death would be life for everyone. Therefore he wanted him to come down from the cross, and made the Pharisees promise that they would believe in him, that through the ₃₅ promise of their faith he might gain what he wanted. But our Lord,

---

[1] *Syriac* : himself.   —   [2] *Mt.*, 27, 40.   —   [3] lifeless *corr.*   —   [4] *Ps.*, 67, 19.   —
[5] *Mt.*, 27, 42.

who in truth is Saviour, who does not seek what is good for himself but what is in our interest, wished to be known as Saviour, not by preserving himself but by saving all creation. Nor is a doctor known to be a doctor by the fact that he is healthy, but when he shows proof of
5 his skill among the sick. And the sun is not known to be shining when it checks its rays, but when it illuminates creation and dispels darkness with its rays. In this way too, our Saviour did not save himself — as Saviour he had no need of salvation — but he wished to be known from (his) help and salvation to others. And he did not wish to be
10 believed to be Son by descending from the cross; but by the fact that he remained on it, his death rather gained for men faith and salvation. But his descent from the cross would have been of no avail; because while he was on the cross graves were opened, and the dead in them arose, and the robber who was hanging believed in him, that he might
15 show that he was Saviour; and faith brought fruit. At these things the devil was truly amazed, and justly despair seized him. He saw that he had lost the thief on the cross; and him whom formerly he had persuaded to be a thief and robber he saw believing on the cross, and him who once was a blasphemer now suddenly become a worshipper of
20 our Saviour, and reproving the other thief — that is Satan who was forceful in him. And again he saw him who had been condemned to death as a thief, transferred to paradise as a believer.

    * 24 He saw that all his armament had fallen and all the various * p. 121 kinds of his stratagems foiled by our Saviour, as it is written : « He
25 destroyed the armament of the enemy and overthrew the cities [1] ». And therefore he was very troubled and consumed by despair. He tried again to give our Saviour vinegar mixed with gall, yet it escaped his notice that this worked against himself. But the bitterness of the anger of the transgression of the commandment which had hold of all
30 he gave to our Saviour to drink. But the latter, accepting it, consumed it completely, that instead of vinegar he might give as drink wine which wisdom had mixed; and instead of gall might grant us words much sweeter than honey and honeycomb; and instead of what he tasted, he said : « Taste and see that the Lord is sweet [2] ».
35 And when again from this too the devil was shamed and fell, the suspicion seized him, who saw the greatness of these things, that he was not fighting with a man but with God. And he saw that he was

---

[1] *Ps.*, 9, 7. — [2] *Ps.*, 33, 9.

they come like rulers to maidens sounding lyres [1] », and those who had
been liberated rejoicing and saying : « When the Lord brings back the
captivity of Sion, we shall be like those who rejoice ; then will our
mouth be filled with joy and our tongue with thanksgiving [2] ». And
the angels again and all the powers of heaven were praising and saying : 5
« Glory to God in the heights, and peace and goodwill on earth to men [3] ».
And they met the maidens' souls ; and these souls again ran with the
angels ; and the patriarchs too ascended with joy, and with the sounds
of lyres rejoiced in the victory won over death.

And as to David after Goliath fell, those rejoicing with lyres went 10
out and met him and said : « David has slain with his myriads [4] »,
so was it at the death of our Saviour. When he arose, everyone met him
with lyres and songs and torches of light ; and everyone said to his
* p. 125 companion : « Come, let us rejoice in the Lord, and praise the God * of
Jacob [5] ». Others rejoiced and said : « I ascended to the height, and 15
took captivity captive, and took gifts to men [6] ». Some called the
majority and urged them to this sight, and said : « Praise the Lord, all
the earth, and sing to his name [7] », and again : « You have seen the
works of the Lord, that he is fearful in his desires more than the sons
of men, destroying wars to the ends of the earth [8] ». There is no more 20
enmity or war, but everything is at peace, in that the enemy is dead.
And he who formerly was a tyrant, now behold is bound hand and
foot. And those who knew him to be cruel in the beginning and his
proud words, now see him laid low ; and they wonder and say : « How
fell the morning-star which shone at dawn ? [9] » and : « How was shattered 25
and broken the hammer of all the earth ? [10] » And he held everyone in
wonder and great uncertainty. They wondered at seeing the great
tyrant suddenly dead, and were uncertain from what cause this fall
had occurred ; because they did not believe that death was destroyed
by death, nor that such a serpent would be crushed by the cross. And 30
they wondered and said : « How did Babylon fall ? [11] » And they saw
hell despoiled and death destroyed.

28 The wretch looked on these things and heard them and greatly
mourned to see himself despoiled. And he saw those who had been
made to weep by him rejoicing and praising the Lord, and he rent 35

---

[1] *Ps.*, 67, 26. — [2] *Ps.*, 125, 1-2. — [3] *Lk.*, 2, 14. — [4] *1 Kings*, 18, 7. —
[5] *Ps.*, 94, 1. — [6] *Ps.*, 67, 19. — [7] *Ps.*, 65, 1-2. — [8] *Ps.*, 45, 9-10. — [9] *Is.*,
14, 12. [10] *Jer.*, 50, 23. — [11] *Jer.*, 50, 23 ; 51, 8.

himself. And he saw the disgrace and derision that had befallen him, and very grievously he sorrowed; and he was at a loss what to do, save only that he gnashed * his teeth — which the psalmist saw and foretold: * p. 126 « The evil doer will watch the just one, and gnash his teeth over him;
5 but the Lord will mock him [1] ». And again : « The impious one will see and be discomfitted, and will gnash his teeth and be inflamed [2] ». And again he gnashed his teeth in remorse at having at all presumed against our Saviour. For he knew that before this he had ventured against the just, and nothing like this had happened to him. Because he had
10 deceived Abel, and afflicted the patriarchs, he had acted deceitfully against Isaiah, and dishonoured Jeremiah, and tempted Job; and again he had been strong and ruled by death from Adam to Moses. But now that he had presumed against our Saviour, he saw that he himself had died, and was expelled from everything and trampled by
15 everyone.

It was our Saviour's task, not only himself to ravish death, but also to enable us to trample it; and not only to grant us deliverance, but also to destroy him who had enslaved us, that he might no longer have power over us or deceive us. And this by his work he corrected
20 for us. For when he had destroyed death, he handed it over to us that we too might trample it, saying : « Behold I have given you power to trample on all serpents and scorpions and on every power of the enemy [3] ». And again : « You will trample the lion and dragon [4] ». For formerly the serpent had led Eve astray, and by this one's envy death
25 entered the world. And now he is trampled; and if he wishes to deceive, he hears : « Go behind me, Satan [5] », and again : « Our enemy the devil like a lion walks around, and seeks and thirsts to devour our soul [6] ». But now he is trampled with the dragon, and henceforth God will grind him quickly under our feet. He is so despised, that if anyone puts his
30 hand in the hole of an asp * he will not fear. This Isaiah prophesied [7], * p. 127 and the saying is true.

29 A youth is he who has not grown old in wickedness and has not been ravished or enticed by pleasures, and not he who is less than full-grown, but he who has girded himself with chastity beyond the law.
35 And virgins, again, are those who by the precept of chastity trample deceitful and crooked pleasures and do not fear their mortal bites.

---

[1] *Ps*, 36, 12-13. — [2] *Ps*, 111, 10. — [3] *Lk*, 10, 19. — [4] *Ps*, 90, 13. — [5] *Mt*, 16, 23; *Mk*, 8, 33. — [6] *1 Pet*, 5, 8. — [7] Cf *Is*, 11, 8.

idols, like the Lord ? And who saved those who were in subjection to them and were zealous in their service, except Christ, who said : « When I have been raised up from the earth, I shall draw all men towards me ¹ » ? This is in truth wonderful, that although they served idols, he opened the mind of their soul, that they might know that those whom ₅ they formerly supposed to be gods ... ² and they despised him who was crucified as a man, but now recognised him as God. Their teacher is no man but God who sees into the mind.

Truly life-giving and blessed are you, cross of our Saviour. You have exposed death, and destroyed the devil who controlled it. You are the ₁₀ Word and wisdom of the Father, who have shown the face of the crafty one and exposed the trickery of his breast, that we might say : « We are not unaware of his designs ³ ». Good and merciful Lord, who when we were prisoners saved us, and when we were slaves freed us. For we know in truth that we have been freed from slavery to sin in ₁₅ you, Christ, truly the Son of God. You gave us adoption and reconciled us to your Father and destroyed enmity in the flesh. Rich Father and true King, you were impoverished that we might become rich by your poverty ; and you granted us the kingdom of heaven. Son of the Father and creator of the world, you renewed us again and created us ₂₀ * p. 131 for good works. * Light in truth, and radiance of the Father, you gave us light in darkness, and led us when we could not see the light. Form and radiance of the Father, you formed us when we were perishing, and granted us to be in the image. You are the Word of God and truly life, who gave us life when we had died, and clothed us in incorruption. ₂₅ You are the power, in truth, and arm and right-hand of the Father.

You have loosed the pains of death, and have broken the gates of brass and the bolts of iron. You have led the great serpent, who is the devil, by means of your own body in shameful form to the victory of the cross. Both because of you and because of the goodness of your ₃₀ victory, behold we all trample him and we all mock him. For in that he mocked you, there now occurred the beginning of the Lord's creatures, that they might mock him. And when he cast you down, it was for everyone a wonder, that all might say : « How the morning-star has fallen from heaven, who shone in the dawn ⁴ ». And in that you took ₃₅ our autograph from him and fixed it to the cross, we all mock him and

---

¹ *Jn.*, 12, 32. — ² Some words have dropped out here. — ³ *2 Cor.*, 2, 11. — ⁴ *Is.*, 14, 12.

say : « How has the avenger become quiet and the inciter come to nought. And God has broken the yoke of the unrighteous. Now below him will be spread decay and putrefaction, and his covering will be tape-worm [6] », that henceforth no one may fear the dragon but worship
5 you, and through you your Father.

32 Thus when our Lord arose, he terrified death and freed us from it. But the Jews, neither when they saw these things were they ashamed, nor did they know when presuming against our Saviour that they were doing these things against themselves, and when they
10 handed him over were inviting the delivery of Jerusalem, as Jeremiah the prophet said : « Jerusalem will indeed be handed over into the hands of Nebuchadnezzar king of Babylon [2] ». Nor again did they see *   * p. 132 that when they were unwilling to be enslaved to our Lord, they enslaved themselves and became slaves and servants to the devil by
15 (their) deceit against our Saviour. And when they requested Barabbas and wished to kill our Lord, they resembled Barabbas in the way of their lives and ventured to murder and blood. And they rejected from themselves light and truth and all those things which Christ is, as Isaiah said : « Behold the Lord Sabaoth will take from Juda and
20 from Jerusalem, that are strong and powerful, the power of bread and the power of water, and the champion and mighty one and warrior, and judge and prophet, and representative and elder, and leader of fifty and wonderful counsellor and intelligent hearer ; and I shall set up young men as their heads, and scoffers will rule over them [3] ». The
25 Jews mocked our Lord and did not know that they were fulfilling the prophetic saying against themselves, which says : « Scoffers will rule over them ».

And this is the wonder of our Saviour's, that when he was crucified he suffered on behalf of humanity, and mocked death, and fulfilled
30 against the Jews what is written, because light too was taken from them. It is written in Jeremiah : « This word that was with Jeremiah before all the people of Juda [4] », and again he adds, saying : « I shall take from them the voice of delight and the voice of rejoicing, the voice of the bridegroom and the voice of the bride, the fragrance of
35 spices and the light of the torch [5] ». When they handed over our Saviour to the Gentiles, they did not know nor did they understand, that

---

[1] Is., 14, 4, 5, 11. — [2] Jer., 32, 4. — [3] Is., 3, 1-4. — [4] Jer., 25, 1. —
[5] Jer,. 25, 10.

they too after a little would be profaned among the Gentiles, and strangers would enter their inheritance, as it is written : « God, the Gentiles have entered your inheritance and have polluted your holy temple; they have made Jerusalem into a fruit-store [1] ». When they denied Christ to be their king, they did not know that they would be [5] *p. 133 alienated from * the honour of king David. For him was kept the kingdom of David, because it remained up to the coming of our Saviour, in that Jacob the patriarch bore witness and said : « There shall not be wanting a ruler for Juda nor a restorer from his loins, until there come he for whom it is laid up; and he is the expectation of the Gentiles [2] ». [10]

And when they stripped him and smote him, they did not know that they were stripped of him and were mourning for themselves. Our Lord said concerning them : « I shall take my garment from her and my clothes, lest she hide her nakedness [3] ». And again : « He mourned and wept and walked hastily, and made weeping like the [15] dragon and lamentation like the daughters of jackals [4] ». And they dressed him in a scarlet tunic, and did not know that they had fulfilled the accusation of the Spirit against themselves, who said : «Your hands are full of blood [5] ». And because they rejoiced again in having placed a crown of thorns on our Saviour, they were rightly blinded [20] and did not understand that which is written : « Stand in awe and be distressed, those who trust and are arrogant. Strip naked, put sackcloth round your loins, and on your breast make lamentation for the field of desire and the offspring of the vine. The land of my people will produce thorns and grass; and from every house joy will be cast out [6] ». They [25] mocked our Saviour, saying : « If you are the Son of God [7] », and they did not understand and see that they were being expelled from adoption, according to the testimony of our Lord, who says : « Sons I have begotten and raised up, but they dealt falsely [8] », and : « Behold your desolate house will be taken from you [9] ». [30]

They gave him vinegar and gall to drink; and in that were very *p. 134 blind * and did not realise that God [10] had brought the vine out of Egypt and planted it, and waited to take from them grapes and wine. But the fools, instead of wine stretched out vinegar to him; and instead of grapes, gall. And this is an indication of their wickedness, showing [35]

---

[1] *Ps., 78, 1.* — [2] *Gen., 49, 10.* — [3] *Hos., 2, 9.* — [4] *Micah, 1, 8.* — [5] *Is., 1, 15.* — [6] *Is., 32, 11-13.* — [7] *Mt., 4, 3; 27, 40; Lk., 4, 3, 9.* — [8] *Is., 1, 2.* — [8] *Mt., 23, 38.* — [10] For a fragment in C see *Appendix*, p. 108.

them to resemble the Sodomites, because their grapes too were gall
as it is written in *Deuteronomy* [1]. Therefore our Saviour also, since he
knew what would be done by them — that is fruits of gall — predicted
to them through the parable of the vineyard that the kingdom of God
5 would be taken from them and given to the people that produces
fruit worthy of it. With that again, they also divided his garments,
and did not realise that the division would be against themselves
among the Gentiles and according to the saying of the prophet who
declared : « Behold the days are coming, says the Lord, and your spoil
10 will be divided among you, and I shall gather all the Gentiles for war
against Israel ; and your cities will be subdued and your houses will be
plundered, and your women will be defiled [2] », and : « Pollution will
consume your inheritance [3] ». And again according to Micah who says :
« This parable will be brought against you, and you will make mourning
15 with a sad voice and say : We have been made most miserable, because
of the inheritance of my people which has been divided with a measuring-line, and there is no-one who will prevent this and turn it away [4] ».

To speak generally : because they presumed against our Saviour,
they called upon themselves the day which the prophet foretold,
20 « the day of judgement for the Lord and retribution of judgement.
Your fields will be turned to plunder, and your land will burn like pitch
day and night and will not be extinguished, and its smoke will rise
above generations and will lay them waste. And its desolation will last
a long time. And there will nest in it birds and snakes and vipers, and
25 ravens * will dwell in it. And the dividers of the land will raise against it   * p. 135
a measuring-line. And mountain asses will dwell in it. And its kings and
nobles and judges will go to destruction. And thorns will flourish in it.
And in its palaces will enter thistles. And it will become a dwelling-
place for jackals, and a lodging-place for sparrows. And demons will
30 meet the mountain asses and they will feed with each other and take
rest in it, as they found for themselves rest in it. And the vipers will
nest in it, for the land found its children in safety [5] ».

33 These things happened to the Jews, who supposed that they had
killed our Lord ; these things they called upon themselves and by them
35 they were condemned, because they had cried out against our Saviour
that he be crucified. Let he who wishes come forward and be judge.

---

[1] Cf. *Deut.*, 32, 32. — [2] *Zech.*, 14, 1-2. — [3] *Hos.*, 5, 7. — [4] *Micah*, 2, 4. —
[5] *Is.*, 34, 8-15.

Not from unkown facts but from events performed and which took place let him reckon the truth. And let him see what is the fruit of the Lord's death, and what again is the profit of the Jews' trickery. The death of our Saviour has freed the whole world and taught the Gentiles that he is God; but the anger of the Jews destroyed them and over- 5 turned their cities and blinded their knowledge of God. The death of our Lord gave life to the dead; but the deceit of the Jews alienated them from life, and they are dead by separation from the Lord. The cross of our Saviour peopled the church of the Gentiles, which was desolated and deserted; but the Jews through their wickedness have 10 been estranged from the whole world, and now they have no city. The death of our Saviour has opened the kingdom of heaven and increased blessings; but the anger of the Jews both destroyed their kings and brought down their nobles.

In addition to these things, the cross of our Saviour mingled angels 15 with men, and Christ became the mediator of their reconciliation and * p. 136 peace; but the Jews by their trickery gained the advantage * of dwelling with the demons, and now in the manner of their lives they consort with sirens and vipers and birds. Instead of the law, they behave lawlessly; instead of gentleness and humility their passion is like that 20 of serpents and vipers; and altogether, there is nothing among them that will not bring death upon them. So is not the whole congregation of the Pharisees worthy to be condemned to death, in that they honoured love of the Jews rather than worshipping the cross? They will have reconciliation with the evil-doers, and will say like Paul : 25 « I consider everything loss that I may gain Christ [1] ». Therefore he boasted in the cross and said : « Let it not happen that I boast save in the cross of our Lord Jesus Christ, through whom the world is crucified to me and I am crucified to the world [2] ». Therefore also our Lord said : « Who does not take up his cross and follow me is not worthy to be a 30 disciple of mine [3] ».

34 So we need great caution lest we take up the cross like the Jews and not like Paul, who as a sign of victory over sin bore it — but the Jews in order to condemn our Saviour by it. Therefore we need care and vigilance, lest accusing the Jews of what they did, we be found 35 ourselves to be acting against our Saviour. For there are many that worship him yet do not behave in a fitting way, and are unmindful

[1] *Phil.*, *3, 8.* — [2] *Gal.*, *6, 14.* — [3] *Mt.*, *10, 38; Lk.*, *14, 27.*

that thereby they become guilty of our Saviour's death. « Everyone
who eats this bread and drinks the cup of the Lord when unworthy,
is guilty of the body and blood of the Lord [1] », according to the testimony of the apostle. Thus he who hates his brother does not love the
5 Lord; but as the Jews, so also he. He who oppresses a poor man and
despises him, he too acts like the Jews who * dishonoured our Lord.   * p. 137
For Solomon said : « Who oppresses the poor man provokes the anger
of his creator [2] ». And he who allows the poor man to be hungry and
thirsty and naked resembles the Jews, who stripped our Saviour and
10 gave him vinegar to drink and gall to eat. And he who takes a bribe
for an innocent man is nothing other than Judas, who sold our Lord
who is justice and righteousness. And he who does not judge the
orphans or render to the widow correct judgment, he is the one who
acted deceitfully towards our Lord and fabricated charges against him.
15 And the sum of all these : whatever anyone wishes to do to his neighbour is reckoned against our Lord, who descended from his heaven
and died on our behalf, as he said in the gospel : « Just as anyone does
to one of these small ones who believe in me, he does it to me [3] ».

And again, the other thing that must be known and which should
20 be kept : he who prostitutes himself is destroyed. Like the Jews he
abuses the temple — that is the body of our Saviour. « For he who
destroys the temple of God, he is destroyed by God [4] », as Paul writes.
And he over whom sin reigns is like the Jews who said of our Lord :
« We have no king except Caesar [5] ». Let him who is held in the grip of
25 pleasures not be unaware that he too like the Jews asks for Barabbas
and kills our Lord. Because the Jews also loved the way of Barabbas'
wickedness and banished virtue. Let him who is not strong in his faith
also know that he is just like those who did not believe and said : « If
you are the Son of God, come down from the cross and we shall believe
30 in you [6] ». And this they said from unbelief.

So we must both believe and show a way of life that befits faith, as
Paul said : « Be imitators of me, * as I am also of Christ [7] ». And let us   * p. 138
refuse love for the Jews, and let us flee from their unbelief and their
mocking and their sneering, and from fables and endless stories, which
35 give rise to disputes and not edification and faith in God. Let us all
hold the cross and live lives worthy of it, and let us say with Paul :

---

[1] *1 Cor.*, 11, 27. — [2] *Prov.*, 14, 31. — [3] *Mt.*, 25, 40. — [4] *1 Cor., 3, 17.* —
[5] *Jn.*, 19, 15. — [6] *Mt., 27, 42.* — [7] *1 Cor., 4, 16.*

« Let it not be that we boast except in the cross of our Lord Jesus Christ [1] », that believing and living we may know the ascension of our Lord to heaven and his sitting at the right hand of his majesty, and see again both the obedience of the angels and his glorious second coming, which the angels foretell and the righteous praise ; and all those who see rejoice and delight in Christ, through whom (be) glory and power to the Father and the holy Spirit, for ever and ever, Amen.

And on the sinner who scribbled (this) may there be the mercy of Christ, Amen.

The end of the discourse of Athanasius on the cross.

---

[1] *Gal.*, 6, *14*.

1 Those who have once turned from pagan error and have recognised the one and only truly God of all, must no more approach creation
5 nor deify creation and worship it besides the creator, « who is blessed
for ever and ever [2] ».In the same way also, those who have turned from
Jewish unbelief, and have blamed them as lacking in intelligence and [3]
infidels and have believed in the Lord Jesus Christ, and have understood
that God is witnessed [4] everywhere and is recognised by power and
10 signs and divine works and the Lord's coming — they must no longer
fall on a simple and common man because of the outer appearance,
nor define in visible form his invisible nature, nor because of the body
and bodily sufferings suppose [5] him to be entirely a man and passible
like one of those of our ilk. For these are the wickednesses of the Jews,
15 which have overturned their faith and shown them to be fighters
with God. Even now some have this error, having pagan and Jewish
illnesses [6], since they do not believe nor do they accept at all that God
became incarnate; but rather by human thoughts * and pagan wisdom * p. 140
they wish to know and comprehend the greatest and incomprehensible
20 things. How, they say, was the bodiless born; and how and where
came forth he who is everywhere and holds everything and fills everything? And from this « where » and « how » they have been reduced to
unbelief; and [7] instead of a birth they have fashioned a making, and
instead of a coming forth they have set up creation and a passage.
25 **2** Thus again also [8] concerning the incarnation : How, they say,
is God incarnate, how is he incorporate, how is the uncontainable fitted
to a small body, and how is the uncreated united to a creature, and ⌐the
limited to the unlimited [9]; how too was in a part the great and un-
measurable and indivisible ? For either the great was restrained in a
30 small place, or the small became great or received a part of the Godhead and not the entirety — which is impiety. And from this « how »

---

[1] + the same A. — [2] *Rom.*, 1, *15.* — [3] and *om.* A. — [4] worshipped A. —
[5] count A. — [6] illness A. — [7] and *om.* A. — [8] also *om.* B. — [9] the unlimited to the limited A.

and « in what way » and « with what connection » these too have turned
to unbelief. And they have prepared an indwelling instead of the
incarnation, and instead of the union and fitting together a human
operation, and instead of the one hypostasis of our Lord Jesus Christ
two hypostases and persons, and instead of the holy Trinity unfittingly ₅
and lawlessly they have thought up a quaternity. Unfittingly, as they
join a man to God and number a servant with the Lord and join a
created person to the uncreated person. And lawlessly, as they make
the single hypostasis two, introducing into the Trinity a fourth hypostasis, which is altogether foreign and different in origin and last and ₁₀
endmost [1] and least of all rational creatures.

* p. 141   Again, if you carefully consider and care to examine * the scriptures [2]
you will find them casting our Lord Jesus Christ, who is to be worshipped, outside the holy Trinity as a man, a servant, who is not to be
worshipped but is rather a worshipper and fearer with everyone, ₁₅
and subordinate to the holy Trinity; as Marcellus and Paul of Samosata wickedly expound the divine and apostolic writing, introducing
into it their own opinion. « For when everything will be subjected to
him, then also the Son [3], that is [4] the man who was assumed, will be
subjected to him who subjects everything to himself, that he may ₂₀
become God, as he was [5] before the incarnation [6] incorporeally in
everything [7] », having no body. And the man who was assumed will
be numbered with all and among all, approaching and subjected and
worshipping God. Observe into what great stupidity they have fallen,
they who were considered wise; to what unbelief and insanity have they ₂₅
been reduced, that they invent non-existent things and create fancies
and utter fables.

3   Not only did they not wish to approach the faith, but they also
invented deception and contrived cunning and fashioned stupid and
ignorant queries for the deception of many, fashioning [8] a rebellion ₃₀
of impiety but taking no thought for the future. For if they had anti-
cipated the future, if they had believed in the coming and [9] the judgement of God or feared the torment, they would have approached the
faith, they would also have believed the gospels, they would have been
in accord with the apostles rather than with human reasonings. For ₃₅
once the apostles had set out they preached Christ the Son of God,

---

[1] other B.   —   [2] scripture A.   —   [3] creature A.   —   [4] + in B.   —   [5] is A.   —
[6] assumption A.   —   [7] *1 Cor.*, 15, 28.   —   [8] choosing A.   —   [8] of A.

agreeing with and in accordance with each other. He * who was born in   * p. 142
Bethlehem from the seed of David in the flesh, who was made like men
and crucified for men in the days of Pontius Pilate — him they said
to be God and the same to be man, the Son of God and the same a son
5 of man, from heaven and the same from earth, impassible and the
same passible, not one and another, not two persons and hypostases,
nor two adorations.

What need was there to investigate and quarrel with words ? It is
better to believe and fear and worship in silence. I know him to be
10 God, impassible, truly from heaven ; I know him to be ⌜from the seed of
David in the flesh [1], a passible man from earth. I do not investigate
how the same one is passible and how he is impassible, how he is God
and how man, lest investigating this « how » and enquiring into the
« mode », I fall from the blessing laid up for us [2]. For in the first place
15 we must believe and praise, and secondly ask from above for confirmation of these things, and not acquire this from below, from flesh and
blood, but from divine and heavenly revelation. « For blessed are you,
Simon son of Jona, because flesh and blood have not revealed to you,
but my Father who is in heaven [3] », and : « You are Kepha, and on this
20 rock I shall build my church, and the gates of hell will not prevail
against it [4] ». Trustworthy is the saying and unshakeable the promise :
the church is unconquerable even if the gates of hell wax strong, even
if hell is shaken, even if the holders of the world of darkness who are in
it (are also shaken). Take courage in him who said : « Take courage, I
25 have conquered the world [5], and sufferings in like fashion I have
conquered ». Because the Lord of this, although he suffered, rather * was   * p. 143
victorious, and although he was crucified he redeemed, and although
he died he gave life. You see and hear the same to be God as also man.
For if he were only God, how would he have suffered, how would he
30 have been crucified and died ? For these things are foreign to God.
And if he were only a man, how would he have conquered through
suffering, have redeemed, have given life ? These things are above a
man. But he suffers and redeems and conquered through sufferings ;
the same is God, and [6] the same man, who is from two together [7],
35 and ⌜from two [8] one.

---

[1] in the flesh from the seed of the house of David A.   —   [2] me B.   —   [3] *Mt.*, 16,
17. —   [4] *Mt.*, 16, *18.* —   [5] *Jn.*, 16, *33.* —   [6] and *om.* A. —   [7] one A. —   [8] in
both A.

So we rejoice at the birth of Christ; we do not rejoice with human joy — as men rejoice when a son is born and celebrate the feast of the birth -- but we rejoice at the manifestation of Christ and the shining forth of the divine light; not a comrade of slavery but the [1] Saviour, as the apostle said. So what was the use of these things by which he was 5 born in a more divine way and not as men? And he grew up divinely ⌐rather than [2] like us. So in the form of the flesh Christ was baptised in water with the Jews, and he who baptised was John, and the river was the Jordan which washed the divine body, and (there occurred) the coming of the Spirit from heaven onto the pure body of Christ, 10 from which there also passes to us purification [3] in the same way, in order that we also may follow him, fulfilling all righteousness and purified in the Lord, to whom be glory for ever [4]. Amen.

End ⌐of the discourse of Athanasius on the faith [5].

---

[1] our A. — [2] rather than *om.* B. — [3] thus A. — [4] + and ever A. — [5] of ... faith *om.* A.

ON THE DIVINE INCARNATION OF GOD THE WORD, WHICH AGREES WITH
THAT OF THE HOLY SYNOD (HELD) IN NICAEA [2].

We confess [3] the Son of God, who before worlds was eternally born;
who at the end of ages for our salvation was born in the flesh from
Mary, as the divine apostle teaches, saying : « When the completion
of times arrived, God sent his Son, born of a woman [4] ». And the same
is Son of God and God in the Spirit, but son of man in the flesh. Not
two natures [5], one Son, one worshipped and the other not worshipped;
but one nature [6] of God the Word who is incarnate and worshipped
with his flesh in one adoration. Nor two sons, one the true and worship-
ful Son of God, but the other from Mary a man not to be worshipped,
who by grace became the Son of God, like men; but he who is from
God and God, as I said, is one Son of God and God. And it was not
another who was also [7] born of Mary in the flesh in the latter days. As
also the angel said to Mary the mother of God when she asked : « How
will this be, as I have not known a man ? » « The holy Spirit will come [8]
over you, * and the power of the Highest will rest upon you; and there-   * p. 148
fore he who is born from you is holy. He will be called the Son of
God [9] ».

So he who was born from the virgin Mary is Son of God by nature,
and true God, and ⌜did not become (so) [10] by grace or by participation.
In the flesh only he is man from Mary, but in the Spirit the same is
Son of God ⌜and God [11], who suffered our passions ⌜in the flesh [12], as
it is written : « Christ suffered for us in the flesh [13] ». And again : « For
he who did not spare his own Son, but handed him over for all of us [14] ».
For he remained impassible and unchangeable in Godhead [15], according
to what is said by [16] the prophet : « I am God [17] and have not changep [18] ».
⌜And he died [19] our death in the flesh for our sins, that he might destroy

[1] The same saint Athanasius A. — [2] + Saint Cyril quotes the same exposition in the
first discourse to Theodorus A. — [3] For a fragment in S see *Appendix*, p. 107. — [4] *Gal.*,
4, 4. — [5] hypostases A. — [6] hypostasis A. — [7] who also] although A. — [8] S
masc.; A fem. — [9] *Lk.*, 1, 34-35. — [10] not A. — [11] and God *om.* A. — [12] in
the flesh *om.* S. — [13] *1 Pet.*, 4, 1. — [14] *Rom.*, 8, 32. — [15] in his Godhead A.
[16] in A. — [17] God *om.* A. — [18] *Mal.*, 3, 6. — [19] who died S.

* APPENDIX

(fragments too long for inclusion in the notes)

Contra Apollinarium I

§5 (S f.5v, col. 3). For concerning the flesh and bones and body and
soul — when our Lord said that his soul was troubled and disturbed ₅
and sad, no one says that these are (features) of the godhead by nature,
but they became God's by nature, when the Word consented to submit
to human birth, in order to correct in himself his own creation which
had been dissolved in sin and corruption and death. And he effected
the condemnation of sin on earth, and the destruction of the curse on ₁₀
the cross ¹, and the eradication of corruption in the tomb, and the
loosing of death in hell. He passed through every place in order to
complete the salvation of everyone, showing in himself the form of our
own image. But why was necessary for God ... birth from a woman,
and for the creator of worlds growth in stature and the numbering of ₁₅
years, or again the cross or tomb, to which we were subject, unless he
had wished to give us life through our own form, and call (us) to the
likeness and resemblance of the perfect image ?

§7 (S f.6r, col. 1). Certainly Adam brought down to the condemnation
... of death a body that was sinless and innocent. But Christ showed ₂₀
it to be incorruptible and the solvent of death ... he has power on
earth to forgive sins, and to show incorruptibility from the tomb, * and
by his entrance to hell to loose death ² and announce to all the resurrection.

§18 (S f.5v, col. 2). Of blessed Athanasius, bishop of Alexandria, ₂₅
from the discourse against Apollinarius.
In the dispensation on the cross one can also understand what is
being said. How our Lord showed the confirmation of the flesh by the
coming-forth of the blood, and indicated by the adding of water the
unsullied purity and that the body was God's. And when he cried out ₃₀
and bent his head and gave up the spirit, which was within his own

---

¹ + and eradiction of the curse on the cross *underlined.* — ² *Syriac* : form.

body, he indicated the soul. Concerning this he also said : « I lay it
down for my sheep [1] ». So no one says that the leaving of the spirit is
the removal of the godhead, but the separation of the soul. For if by
the removal of the godhead were effected the death and mortality of
5 the body, then he died his own death and not ours. And how did he
go down to hell in open godhead ? So where is the soul which our Lord
promised that he would lay down for his sheep, concerning which the
prophets too had foretold ? But if a separation of the soul occurred,
therefore it is said that he accepted our death — that is he condescended
10 to our dissolution, as also to birth.

§20 (S f.77v, col. 2). How do you seek to say these things, trafficking
in the life of God with created words ? The church has not so received,
nor so believes. But as it is written, God who is with God before ages,
at the end of ages came, and was born a son of man from the holy virgin
15 and a holy Father and the holy Spirit, as it is written : « until she
gave birth to her first-born son [2] », « that he might be first-born * among   * p. 153
many brothers [3] », who is true God, in order to suffer on our behalf as
a man, and save us from suffering and death as God.

20 *De Incarnatione Dei Verbi*

(S f.48v, col. 3). Of blessed Athanasius, from the discourse on the
Incarnation.
For we confess, he said, both that he is the Son of God and God in
the Spirit, and the son of man in the flesh. Not two natures to the one
25 Son, one worshipped, and the other not worshipped; but one nature
of God the Word incarnate and worshipped with his flesh in one
adoration.

De Passione et Cruce

§12 (E f.8r). Of saint Athanasius, patriarch of Alexandria, from the
30 discourse on the saving cross.
Hence in no other place does he suffer, and in no other place is he
crucified, except in the place of the skull, which the teachers of the
Hebrews say is the tomb of Adam. For they aver that Adam was
buried there after the curse. If this is so, I am amazed at the suitability
35 of the passion. For it was fitting for the Lord, when he wished to renew

---

[1] *Jn.*, 10, *15.* — [2] *Lk.*, 2, 7. — [3] *Rom*, 8, 29.

the first Adam, to suffer in that place, that when he had loosed the former's curse, he might remove it from the whole race. And because Adam heard : « Dust you are and to dust you will return [1] », therefore he again was buried there, in order that finding Adam there, he might loose the curse. For instead of « dust you are and to dust you will return », he would henceforth say : « Awake, sleeper, and rise from the house of the dead, and Christ will illuminate you ». And again : « Arise and follow, cleave to me, that you no longer be buried in the earth, but rise to heaven ».

* p. 154   * §13 (S f.6v, col. 2). Of the same from the discourse on the cross.
And the fact that Pilate should thus make excuse, was nothing else to believe except that he who was being judged was God. Thus when he was being judged by Pilate, he spoke to the latter's wife, that by his silence he would be judged by his fortitude, but by his speech it would be known that he was judging not the man but God. So he who was judging was afraid of him who was being judged, and rather he was judged by fear of the one judged ... the judge (?) wondered at the Lord, and therefore ... his hands, saying : « I am innocent of the blood of this (man) [2] ».

§25 (S f.6v, col. 3). For he was not slain in any other place except in the rib, from which flowed blood and water ; that because previously through the woman created from the rib error had entered, so through the rib of the second Adam salvation ... that this first ... salvation through the blood, but purification through the water. But this did not ... come to pass for the devil. For the death which he feared ... our Lord died, and he was despoiled. And when he supposed that he held Christ in death, rather he was seen to be dead. And when he boasted that he had ambushed the man, he caused him to be known to be God.

§32 (C f.108r). Section from the homily on the cross and passion of the Lord, composed by Saint Athanasius, bishop of Alexandria.
For God brought the vine out of Egypt and planted it, and waited to take from them fruit of grapes and wine. But the fools instead of wine gave vinegar, and instead of grapes, gall ; showing an indication of * p. 155 their wickedness like the Sodomites, because their grapes * are gall, as it is written in *Deuteronomy* [3]. So therefore the Lord and our Saviour, knowing such fruit which would be done by them, previously told

---

[1] *Gen., 3, 19.* — [2] *Mt., 27, 24.* — [3] Cf. *Deut., 32, 32.*

them the parable of the vineyard — that the kindgom of God would
be taken from them and given to the people that worked its fruit.
With that they divided his garments among the gaolers, although they
did not see the division that would occur against themselves among
5 the Gentiles. For the prophet said : « Behold the days will come, says
the Lord, and your spoil will be divided among you, and I shall gather
all the Gentiles for war against Israel. And cities will be captured, and
houses will be pillaged, and women will be defiled [1] ». And again :
« Pollution will consume their inheritance [2] ». And as Micah said : « In
10 that day the parable will be brought against you, and we shall mourn
over you with a cry, saying : we have been made most miserable. The
portion of my people has been divided with a measuring-line, and
there was no one who will prevent this from turning away. Your fields
have been divided [3] ».

15   And speaking generally : since they presumed against the Lord,
they call upon themselves the day which the prophet too had foretold.
« For the day of judgement for the Lord and retribution of judgement
of Sion. And her fields will be turned to plunder, and her land will
burn like pitch day and night and will not be extinguished. And its
20 smoke will rise upwards and destroy the thistles, and it will destroy
many times. And in it will dwell birds and vipers and asps and [4]
crows. And they will raise against it a geometric measuring line of
desolation. And ass-centaurs (ὀνοκένταυροι) will dwell in it. And its
heads will be no more. For its kings and nobles will go to destruction.
25 And there will flourish in their cities and its fortresses thorny trees.
And it will become a dwelling-place for jackals and a lodge for sparrows. And demons will meet the ass-centaurs and they will cry out to
each other, * as there the ass-centaurs will rest. For there they found   * p. 156
rest for themselves. And the vipers will pervade there. And the land
30 preserved its children securely [5] ».

33   These things the Jews suffered, since they supposed they were
killing the Lord. These things they called upon themselves, since they
cried out against the Saviour. By these things they were condemned,
since they wished to judge the Lord. For if he who wishes to be judge
35 comes forward, he will reckon the truth not from unknown facts, but
from the events which were performed; and he will observe what is

---

[1] *Zech.*, 14, 1-2. — [2] *Hos.*, 5, 7. — [3] *Micah, 2, 4.* — [4] *Syriac* : of. — [5] *Is.,*
34, 8-15.

the fruit of the Lord's death, and what is the profit of the Jews'
mischief. For the death of the Saviour freed the world, and taught
God to the Gentiles; but the anger of the Jews destroyed with the
Jews themselves their city, and blinded them from the knowledge of
God. And the death of the Lord also gave life to the dead, but the ₅
mischief of the Jews deprived them of life. And now they are dead and
without the Lord. And the cross of the Saviour peopled the church of
the Gentiles, which was desolated. But the Jews by their wickedness
have expelled themselves from the world, and now they have no city.
And again the death of the Saviour showed the kingdom of heaven, ₁₀
but the Jews by (their) rage destroyed their kings and removed their
nobles.

In addition to these things, the cross of the Lord joined the angels to
men, and Christ became the mediator of their reconciliation. The Jews,
working injury, gained a dwelling-place with the demons. And the ₁₅
death of the Lord cleared away the irrationality of men concerning
sin. But the Jews had contempt, and now consort in their way of life
with sirens and vipers and sparrows, having thus irregular *mores* like
the ass-centaurs. For instead of the law there is lawlessness among
* p. 157 them; * and instead of gentleness, passion like a snake's. And altogether ₂₀
there is nothing among them that will not work death for them. So
then is it not right that we believe in the death, and abandon the
congregation of the Pharisees ? Is it not right rather to worship the
cross, than to gain the love of the Jews and of the world ? For so
blessed Paul considered everything loss, that he might gain Christ. ₂₅
And therefore he thought the cross to be glory, saying : « Let me not
boast except in the cross of our Lord Jesus Christ, in whom the world
is crucified to me and I to the world ¹ ». And therefore the Lord also
said : « Who does not take up his cross and join me, is not worthy of
me, and cannot become my disciple ² ».   ₃₀

34   But hence great caution is needed lest we take up the cross
like the Jews and not like Paul. For Paul bore it as a sign of victory
over sin, but the Jews in order to reject the Lord. Therefore we must
be careful and vigilant in (our) minds, lest as we accuse the Jews we
do the same things as they against the Lord. For many, although ₃₅
they worship the Lord, yet do not behave as befits him, unaware that
they are guilty of the death of the Saviour. « For everyone who eats

¹ *Gal.*, *6*, *14*. — ² *Mt.*, *10*, *38*; *Lk.*, *14*, *27*.

the bread and drinks the cup of the Lord unworthily, is guilty of the
body of the Lord [1] », testifies the apostle. So also he who hates his
brother does not love the Lord, but as the Jews, so also he hates him.
And he who abhors the poor man and despises him, he too acts like
5 the Jews. This Solomon said : « He who despises the poor man dishonours him who made him [2] ». And he who neglects a poor man who is
hungry and thirsty and naked, resembles the Jews who stripped the
Lord and gave him vinegar and gall to drink. And he who takes a
bribe for * an innocent man is nothing other than Judas, who sold the   * p. 158
10 Lord. For he too sells the justice that is the Lord, as the latter did
Christ. And he who does not judge the orphans and render justice to
widows, is the same as he who injured the Lord and falsely accused
him. And the sum of such things : what a man may do against his
neighbour, these will be reckoned against the Lord, who descended for
15 our sake and died for us. For thus the Lord too said in the gospels :
« Just as you did to one of these little ones, you did it to me [3] ».

And again this must be known and observed : he who prostitutes
himself is destroyed. He too like the Jews dishonours the temple and
body of the Lord. « For, he said, he who destroys the temple of God is
20 destroyed by God [4] », as the apostle wrote. And he over whom sin reigns
resembles the Jews who denied and said : « The Lord is not our king,
but Caesar [5] ». Let him who is held in the grip of pleasures and rather
delights in them, not be unaware that he too like the Jews asks for
Barabbas and kills the Lord. For thus the Jews also, since they loved
25 Barabbas' way of evil, thenceforth banished virtue. And let him who
is not strong in the faith know that he is like those who do not believe
and say : « If he is the Son of God, let him now come down from the
cross and we shall believe in him [6] ». For such things they too said,
disbelieving.

30 So what must we do ? Nothing other than believe in the Lord, and
lead such lives as Paul said : « Be imitators of me, as I am also of
Christ [7] ». And let us turn our faces from love of the Jews, and from
unbelief and derision, and from fables and endless genealogies * that   * p. 159
produce queries rather than a godly way of life in faith. And let us
35 hold the cross and lead lives worthy of it, and let us say the same
words as Paul : « Let me not boast save in the cross of our Lord Jesus

---

[1] *1 Cor.*, 11, 27. — [2] *Prov.*, 14, 31. — [3] *Mt.*, 25, 40. — [4] *1 Cor.*, 3, 17. —
[5] *Jn.*, 19, 15. — [6] *Mt.*, 27, 42. — [7] *1 Cor.*, 4, 16.

Christ [1] ». For leading such lives and believing in the Lord, we shall know his ascension to heaven and his sitting at the right hand of majesty, and we shall see the obedience of the angels. And we shall see again his coming with glory, which the angels foretell, and the saints and righteous praise; and all rejoicing delight and rejoice in Christ, through whom (be) glory and power to the Father, now and always, and for ever and ever, Amen.

The end of the section which is from the homily on the cross of bishop Athanasius, which was translated from Greek into Syriac in the city of Callinicos.

[1] *Gal.*, 6, *14.*

INDEX OF BIBLICAL QUOTATIONS

For the Old Testament the numbering of the Septuagint has been followed. Only direct quotations, not allusions to the biblical text, are listed here. References are to the pages of the English text.